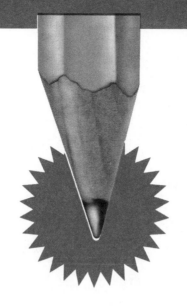

GRAMMARWORK

3

English Exercises
in Context

PAMELA PETERSON BREYER

Longman

Publisher: Mary Jane Peluso
Manager of Development Services: Louisa B. Hellegers
Development Editor: Carol Callahan

Director of Production: Aliza Greenblatt
Editorial Production/Design Manager: Dominick Mosco

Manufacturing Manger: Ray Keating
Production Supervision/Electronic Page Composition: Noël Vreeland Carter
Art Director: Merle Krumper
Cover Design: Marianne Frasco
Electronic Art: Warren Fischbach
Interior Design: Patrice Fodero
Interior Art: Lane Gregory and Dorothea Sierra

Printed in the United States of America
18 19 20 V001 14 13 12

ISBN 0-13-340266-5

To my students at the Braille Institute, Orange County Center

CONTENTS

Present Perfect Tense

Modals and Idiomatic Modals

Passive Voice

Adjective and Adverbs

Comparisons

Noun Clauses

Pronouns

Prepositions

Appendix

Answers to Exercises

INTRODUCTION

Recent studies have shown that students acquire and retain a new language more rapidly and more efficiently when the structure and vocabulary of the language are presented in context; that is, when elements of a lesson, such as grammar and new lexicon, are tied together in some real and meaningful setting. Exercises that present material in such a situational context are referred to as contextualized exercises.

GrammarWork is a series of four contextualized exercise books for students of written English. These books may be used as major texts or as supplementary material, depending on whether a course is nonintensive or intensive. Each exercise in each book presents, as a unit, vocabulary relating to a particular context and structures that are appropriate to that context.

Book One is intended for the beginner: the student enrolled in a first-level English course who has had some exposure to the language. Book Two continues with beginners' material, proceeding from first-level to second-level work. Book Three is designed for the intermediate student, and Book Four contains material appropriate to high-intermediate levels.

The books are organized into grammatical units (i.e., the Verb *To Be*, the Present Continuous, the Simple Present). Each unit contains a variety of exercises with practice in small increments. Most units include more than one exercise on key grammar points, in order to give students sufficient and varied practice. Also included in each unit are review exercises and periodic tense contrast exercises, usually located at the end of the unit.

The pages in each book are, for the most part, divided into three sections:

a. an examination of the structure to be presented (**Grammar**);

b. exercises that enable the student to manipulate that new structure in a contextual setting (**Practice**); and

c. a culminating exercise activity in which the student uses the material in the exercise by applying it to some personal, real-life situation (**Make It Work**).

The **Grammar** section shows the student how to use the structure to be practiced, with diagrams and arrows that should be self-explanatory. Notes of explanation are supplied only when the grammar rule cannot be illustrated clearly.

The **Practice** section consists of a contextualized exercise, usually a page in length and always self-contained; if a context is three pages instead of one, it will be self-contained within those three pages. Thus the teacher can select any exercise or group of exercises he or she considers appropriate for a particular class, lesson, or given time. The teacher can choose to utilize all the exercises in the order presented. The exercises have been arranged in ascending order of difficulty, with structures generally considered to be the easiest for most students presented first.

The exercises are self-contained in that they have been designed for written practice without necessarily being preceded by an introductory teacher's presentation. Since grammatical diagrams have been included and the new vocabulary is usually illustrated or defined, students can work independently, either at home or in class—in pairs or as a group. When students work together in pairs or in groups in the classroom, they should be encouraged to help each other; the teacher, too, can assist by circulating from pair to pair or group to group, guiding and correcting.

The **Make It Work** section enables students to apply what they have been practicing to freer, and sometimes more natural, situations. The activity usually contains a picture cue, a fill-in dialogue, or questions to answer. The purpose of the **Make It Work** section is to provide the student with as real-life a setting as possible.

The perforated answer key can be used by either the student or the teacher. The teacher may choose to withhold the answers on some occasions; on other occasions, the students may use the answer key for self-correction.

ALL THE HOMES ARE 2,000 SQUARE FEET.

Noun Plurals

Verb *To Be*, Simple Present

-s/-es	-ies	-ves	irregular form
bath → bath $\boxed{s}$	study → stud $\boxed{ies}$	shelf → shel $\boxed{ves}$	foot → feet
room → room $\boxed{s}$		knife → kni $\boxed{ves}$	
box → box $\boxed{es}$			
patio → patio $\boxed{s}$			

spelling exception: roof → roofs

PRACTICE

Fill in the blanks with the correct plural form.

Windy Bush is an elegant development of fine homes. All homes in the

development are 2,000 square _____*feet*_____ with two _____

(1. foot)   (2. bath)

and four _____ . All houses have plaster _____ ,

(3. bedroom)   (4. wall)

wooden _____ , _____ , two-car _____ ,

(5. roof)   (6. patio)   (7. garage)

and two _____ . Some models have extra _____ or

(8. fireplace)   (9. den)

_____ . These beautiful homes have built-in _____ ,

(10. study)   (11. bookshelf)

deluxe _____ , built-in _____ on three windows,

(12. oven)   (13. window box)

built-in _____ in all kitchens, and wooden _____

(14. radio)   (15. floor)

throughout each house.

MAKE IT WORK

Tell about your apartment or house.

_____

_____

Equivalent: square foot = .09 meter squared

New Words: plaster = a mixture used on walls to give a smooth surface
built-in = a part of something that cannot be separated from it
wooden = made of wood

SHARKS ARE DANGEROUS.

Noun Plurals

Verb *To Be*

Fish

a shark

a goldfish

Birds

a goose

a pigeon

a parrot

Reptiles

a snake

an alligator

a turtle

Rodents

a mouse

a rat

Insects

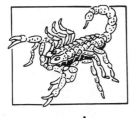
a scorpion

an ant

a wasp

a butterfly

SHARKS ARE DANGEROUS.

Sharks are dangerous.   Mice aren't dangerous.

irregular plurals   Singular and plural forms are the same.

mouse → mice
goose → geese

deer → deer   sheep → sheep   fish → fish

Note: You can make a general statement about a whole class of things using plural statements.

PRACTICE

Look at page 2. Then tell which of the following things are or aren't dangerous. Make plural statements.

1. shark   *Sharks are dangerous.* _____

2. goldfish   _____

3. rattlesnake _____

4. deer   _____

5. goose   _____

6. rat   _____

7. alligator _____

8. wasp   _____

9. butterfly _____

10. sheep   _____

11. scorpion _____

12. mouse   _____

MAKE IT WORK

Name one kind of fish you're afraid of.

_____

Name one kind of reptile you're afraid of.

_____

I'M AFRAID OF DOGS AND MICE.

Countable and Uncountable Nouns

Verb *To Be*, Simple Present

Check the items that best describe you.

I like to eat

vegetables
- ❑ tomatoes
- ❑ corn
- ❑ carrots
- ❑ potatoes
- ❑ spinach
- ❑ broccoli

fruits
- ❑ cherries
- ❑ peaches
- ❑ bananas
- ❑ apples
- ❑ strawberries
- ❑ oranges

snack foods
- ❑ pretzels
- ❑ potato chips
- ❑ cheese
- ❑ candy
- ❑ crackers
- ❑ cookies

I like to drink

beverages
- ❑ wine
- ❑ beer
- ❑ milk
- ❑ coffee
- ❑ soft drinks
- ❑ tea

I like to wear
- ❑ tennis shoes
- ❑ boots
- ❑ high heels
- ❑ suits
- ❑ dresses
- ❑ sunglasses

- ❑ scarves
- ❑ ties
- ❑ jewelry
- ❑ baggy pants
- ❑ T-shirts
- ❑ shorts

I'm allergic to
- ❑ eggs
- ❑ milk
- ❑ cigarette smoke
- ❑ cats
- ❑ grass
- ❑ dust

I'm afraid of
- ❑ dogs
- ❑ sharks
- ❑ snakes
- ❑ mice
- ❑ rats
- ❑ lightning

New Words: allergic = sensitive to certain things you eat or breathe

corn   spinach   broccoli   lightning   dust   smoke

I'M AFRAID OF DOGS AND MICE.

I'm afraid of ┌dogs and mice.┐

I'm afraid of ┌dogs, mice, and lightning.┐

Note: Uncountable nouns have no plural.

broccoli	beer	jewelry	dust
candy	coffee		grass
cheese	milk		lightning
corn	tea		smoke
spinach	wine		

PRACTICE

Give answers for each statement. You can use the items you checked on page 4, or you can add your own items.

1. Name three vegetables you like.

   I like spinach, corn, and peas.

2. Name two vegetables you don't like.

   _____

3. Name two fruits you like.

   _____

4. Name three snack foods you like.

   _____

5. Name three foods you don't like.

   _____

6. Name two beverages you like.

   _____

7. Name three items of clothing you often wear.

   _____

8. Name two items of clothing you don't like to wear.

   _____

9. Name something you're allergic to.

   _____

10. Name three things you're afraid of.

    _____

THE ROSE BUSHES ARE ON SPECIAL.

Nouns in Adjective Position

roses    bushes   rose bushes

Note: Do not add *s* or *es* to nouns used in adjective position.

PRACTICE

Put the words in parentheses in adjective position.

1. Which shoes are on sale today? (tennis) *the tennis shoes* _____

2. Which frames are on sale? (picture) _____

3. Which bushes are reduced? (rose) _____

4. Which tools are on special? (garden) _____

5. Which towels are on sale? (beach) _____

6. Which brushes are on special? (paint) _____

7. Which bowls are reduced? (salad) _____

8. Which tables are on sale? (coffee) _____

9. Which curtains are on special? (shower) _____

10. Which gloves are reduced? (rubber) _____

11. Which glasses are on special? (wine) _____

12. Which clocks are reduced? (wall) _____

MAKE IT WORK

Look at the picture. Then answer the question.

What kind of cards are these?

They're _____

A BUTTERFLY IS AN INSECT.

Articles *A* and *An* for Classifying Statements
Verb *To Be*

| A butterfly is an insect. | An alligator is a reptile. | |

Note: You can make a general statement about a whole class of things using *a* or *an* before the singular form of countable nouns. (See page 3 for irregular plurals.)

PRACTICE

Make the sentences singular.

1. Pigeons are birds.   *A pigeon is a bird.*
2. Sharks are fish.   _____
3. Snakes are reptiles.   _____
4. Butterflies are insects.   _____
5. Geese are birds.   _____
6. Alligators are reptiles.   _____
7. Wasps are insects.   _____
8. Parrots are birds.   _____
9. Mice are rodents.   _____
10. Flies are insects.   _____
11. Turtles are reptiles.   _____
12. Cockroaches are insects.   _____
13. Rats are rodents.   _____
14. Ants are insects.   _____
15. Goldfish are fish.   _____

MAKE IT WORK

Fill in the blanks.

_____ is a beautiful bird.

_____ is a beautiful insect.

_____ is a beautiful fish.

THE PHILIPPINES ARE IN THE PACIFIC OCEAN.

No Article vs. *The* with Place Names

Verb *To Be*

place names without *the*		place names with *the*
continents	Europe Asia	
countries	Japan Vietnam	the United States the Dominican Republic the Netherlands the Philippines
cities	Rome Hong Kong	
states	Texas Indiana	

bodies of water
  rivers
  oceans
 	
  lakes
	
	Lake Michigan
		
		the Nile
		the Atlantic Ocean
		the Mediterranean Sea

islands	Hawaii	the Virgin Islands
beaches	Waikiki Beach	
streets	South Street Fifth Avenue	
colleges and **universities**	 Harvard	 the University of Illinois

Note: Use *the* if a proper noun is plural.

the Philippines   the United States   the West Indies

Use *the* with proper nouns that contain *of*-phrases.

the University of Pennsylvania   the Republic of China

THE PHILIPPINES ARE IN THE PACIFIC OCEAN.

The Philippines are in the Pacific Ocean.

PRACTICE

Look at page 8. Fill in the blanks with either *the* or a line (—) for no article.

1. ___—___ Washington, D.C. is the capital of ___the___ United States.
2. _____ Philippines are in _____ Pacific Ocean.
3. _____ Nile is a river in _____ Africa.
4. _____ Copacabana is a beach in _____ Brazil.
5. _____ University of Southern California is in _____ Los Angeles.
6. _____ Santo Domingo is a city in _____ Dominican Republic.
7. _____ Hawaii is an island in _____ Pacific Ocean.
8. _____ Columbia University is on _____ 116th Street in _____ New York City.
9. _____ Rodeo Drive is in _____ Beverly Hills.
10. _____ Netherlands is in _____ Europe.
11. _____ Republic of China, also called _____ China, is in _____ Asia.
12. _____ Mississippi is a river in _____ United States.
13. _____ Puerto Rico is an island in _____ West Indies in _____ Caribbean Sea.
14. _____ Wall Street is a famous street in _____ New York City.
15. _____ Lake Erie is in _____ Canada and _____ United States.

MAKE IT WORK
Fill in the blanks.

Name a large city in your country. _____

Name a university in your country. _____

Name a lake or river in your country. _____

GO TO THE SUPERMARKET AND GET A LOAF OF BREAD.

Articles A vs. The
Imperatives

> Go to [the] supermarket and get [a] loaf of bread.
>
> Shut [the] curtains. [The] sun is too bright.
>
> Note: Use *the* when you refer to only one of something.
> > the sun   the moon
>
> Use *the* for objects at home or in the community when people
> know which one you are talking about.
> > the supermarket   the refrigerator
>
> Use *a* for unspecified objects. a loaf of bread   a cookie
> Do not use *a* with plural nouns or uncountable nouns.
> > dust   lightning   rain   weather

PRACTICE

Fill in the blanks with *a* or *the*.

1. Go into ___the___ kitchen and get me ___a___ cookie.

2. Please bring me _____ sweater. It's in _____ closet upstairs.

3. Shut _____ curtains. _____ sun is too bright.

4. Go to _____ drugstore and get me _____ bottle of aspirin.

5. Open _____ can of dog food and then feed _____ dog.

6. Go to _____ refrigerator and get me _____ glass of milk.

7. Please answer _____ door. _____ doorbell is ringing.

8. Look at _____ moon. It's _____ beautiful evening.

9. Close _____ windows. _____ rain is coming into
   _____ house.

10. Please bring me _____ pen. It's on _____ counter.

11. Look at _____ clouds in _____ sky. It's going to rain.

12. _____ weather is very cold. Please get me _____ coat.

13. Please clean _____ dust off _____ dining room table.

14. Look at _____ lightning. Please don't go outside.

New Words: cloud   moon   sky

PUERTO RICO IS AN ISLAND.

Review: Articles, Countable and Uncountable Nouns

Verb *To Be*

The	United States is	a	country.
	Broccoli is	a	vegetable.

PRACTICE

Use the words in the chart below. Make singular sentences with *a, an, the*, or no article.

Paris			fruit.
Waikiki			vegetable.
South America			beverage.
Pacific			fish.
apple			insect.
corn	is	a	continent.
Nile		an	country.
shark		the	island.
ant			city.
Puerto Rico			ocean.
Netherlands			river.
coffee			beach.

1. *Paris is a city.*
2. _____
3. _____
4. _____
5. _____
6. _____
7. _____
8. _____
9. _____
10. _____
11. _____
12. _____

Affirmative Statements

Simple Present, Verb *To Be*

PROFILE OF
CHRIS GOLDMAN

1. **Sex**
   - ☑ Male
   - ☐ Female

2. **Age**
   _48_

3. **Height**
   _5'8"_

4. **Weight**
   180 lbs.

5. **Hair**
   - ☑ blond
   - ☐ red
   - ☐ black
   - ☐ brown

6. **Eyes**
   - ☑ blue
   - ☐ green
   - ☐ brown
   - ☐ hazel

7. **Smoking**
   - ☐ smoker
   - ☑ non-smoker

8. **Profession**
   teacher

9. **Salary**
   - ☐ over $20,000 a yr.
   - ☑ over $30,000 a yr.
   - ☐ over $50,000 a yr.
   - ☐ over $100,000 a yr.

10. **Marital Status**
    - ☐ married
    - ☑ single
    - ☐ divorced
    - ☐ separated

11. **Languages**
    - ☑ English
    - ☑ French
    - ☐ Spanish
    - ☐ Other

12. **Preferred Sports**
    tennis
    ping-pong

13. **Hobbies**
    reading

New Words: over $30,000 = more than $30,000
under $30,00 = less than $30,000
non-smoker = a person who doesn't smoke
hazel = light greenish brown

Equivalents: 1 foot = 30.5 centimeters
1 inch = 2.54 centimeters
1 pound = .45 kilogram

Abbreviations: foot = ft. (')
inch = in. (")
pound = lb.

HE MAKES OVER $30,000 A YEAR.

He ⸢'s⸣ 48.   He ⸢weighs⸣ 180 pounds.   He ⸢doesn't smoke.⸣

PRACTICE

Look at page 12. Then make one sentence about Chris Goldman for each category. Use contractions whenever possible.

1. Sex: _He's a male._____
2. Age: _____
3. Height: _____
4. Weight: _____
5. Hair: _____
6. Eyes: _____
7. Smoking: _____
8. Profession: _____
9. Salary: _____
10. Marital Status: _____
11. Languages: _____
12. Preferred Sports: _____
13. Hobbies: _____

MAKE IT WORK

Fill in the driver's license application with information about yourself.

Driver License Application

Date:_____

Name: _____

Address: _____

_____

Sex: _____   Date of Birth: _____

Eyes: _____   Hair: _____

Height: _____   Weight: _____

HOW MUCH DO YOU WEIGH?

WH Questions and Yes-No Questions

Simple Present, Verb *To Be*

> How much do you weigh?
> How tall are you?

PRACTICE

Write some questions that you can ask a classmate. Write one question for each category.

1. Name: *What's your name?* _____
2. Residence: _____
3. Birthplace: _____
4. Age: _____
5. Height: _____
6. Weight: _____
7. Color of Eyes: _____
8. Color of Hair: _____
9. Profession: _____
10. Place of Employment: _____
11. Marital Status: _____
12. Languages: _____
13. Sports: _____
14. Hobbies: _____

MAKE IT WORK

Interview a classmate using the questions above. Then write two sentences about your classmate.

_____

_____

SHE DOESN'T ANSWER THE TELEPHONE.

Simple Form vs. Present Form

Simple Present

simple form	present form
She doesn't answer the telephone.	Her maid answers the telephone.

PRACTICE

Fill in the blanks with the simple form or the present form of the verb.

Marie Moreau is a very famous and very rich person.

1. (get) She doesn't _____*get*_____ up early in the morning.

2. (get) She _____ up whenever she wants to.

3. (clean) She doesn't _____ her house.

4. (clean) Her cleaning woman _____ her house.

5. (fix) She doesn't _____ her own breakfast.

6. (fix) Her maid _____ breakfast for her.

7. (answer) When the doorbell rings, she doesn't _____ the door.

8. (answer) Her butler _____ the door.

9. (get) She doesn't _____ dressed by herself.

10. (help) Her maid _____ her get dressed.

11. (answer) If the telephone rings, she doesn't _____ it.

12. (answer) Her maid _____ the telephone.

13. (drive) She doesn't _____ her car.

14. (drive) Her chauffeur _____ her anywhere she wants to go.

MAKE IT WORK

Complete the sentences with a negative or affirmative verb.

I _____ a cleaning woman.

I _____ my house myself.

New Words: butler = a man who works as a servant in another person's house

chauffeur = a person hired to drive someone's car

SUDDENLY A BIG BAD WOLF JUMPED OUT OF THE BUSHES.

Regular Verbs

Simple Past

SUDDENLY A BIG BAD WOLF JUMPED OUT OF THE BUSHES.

> She decide $\boxed{d}$ to visit her grandmother.
> Suddenly a big bad wolf jump $\boxed{ed}$ out of the bushes.
>
> Note: Add *d* or *ed* to form the past tense.

PRACTICE

Fill in the blanks with the correct past form.

Little Red Riding Hood _____*lived*_____ with her parents in a little
(1. live)

house near the forest. One day Little Red Riding Hood _____
(2. decide)

to visit her grandmother. She _____ some cookies and
(3. bake)

_____ them in her basket. Then she _____
(4. pack)   (5. walk)

through the forest to her grandmother's house.

Suddenly a big bad wolf _____ out of the bushes. The wolf
(6. jump)

_____ her. He _____ her, "Little girl, where are
(7. follow)   (8. ask)

you going?"

"I'm going to visit my sick grandmother," she _____, "and I'm
(9. answer)

taking her some cookies." The wolf was happy. He _____
(10. like)

cookies and little girls.

Finally, Little Red Riding Hood _____ at her grandmother's
(11. arrive)

house. She _____ that the door was open. She
(12. notice)

_____ the house. Her grandmother wasn't there. The wolf was
(13. enter)

there. When she_____ at the wolf, Little Red Riding Hood took
(14. look)

a gun out of her basket and _____ him.
(15. kill)

SHE DIDN'T EXPECT TO SEE THE WOLF.

Past Form vs. Simple Form

Simple Past

> **past form**
>
> She [walked] to her grandmother's house.
>
> **simple form**   **simple form**
>
> She didn't [expect]   to   [see] the wolf.

PRACTICE

Fill in the blanks with the past form or the simple form of the verb.

1. (live) Little Red Riding Hood _____*lived*_____ near the forest.

2. (live) She didn't _____ in a big house.

3. (visit) One day she decided to _____ her grandmother.

4. (live) Her grandmother didn't _____ far away.

5. (walk) She _____ to her grandmother's house.

6. (jump) Suddenly a wolf _____ out of the bushes.

7. (follow) He _____ Little Red Riding Hood.

8. (stop) Little Red Riding Hood didn't _____.

9. (talk) She didn't want to _____ to the wolf.

10. (ask) The wolf _____ her some questions.

11. (want) She didn't _____ to answer his questions.

12. (like) She didn't _____ the wolf.

13. (like) But the wolf _____ her.

14. (walk) When Little Red Riding Hood arrived at her grandmother's house, she _____ into the bedroom.

15. (see) She didn't expect to _____ the wolf.

16. (expect) She _____ to see her grandmother.

17. (reach) She _____ into her basket.

18. (pull) She _____ out a gun.

19. (kill) The wolf didn't _____ her.

20. (kill) She _____ the wolf.

I HEARD A FUNNY JOKE YESTERDAY.

Irregular Past Tense Verbs

When did you last hear a funny joke? I heard a funny joke yesterday.
                                                                      two days ago.

bring → brought	drive → drove	have → had	send → sent
buy → bought	find → found	hear → heard	take → took
catch → caught	give → gave	make → made	write → wrote
do → did	go → went	read → read	

PRACTICE

Answer the questions. Tell about yourself.

1. When did you last read the newspaper?
   I read the newspaper this morning.

2. When did you last give a party?
   _____

3. When did you last make an appointment?
   _____

4. When did you last have a haircut?
   _____

5. When did you last drive a car?
   _____

6. When did you last write a letter?
   _____

7. When did you last take a taxi?
   _____

8. When did you last buy a book?
   _____

9. When did you last catch a cold?
   _____

10. When did you last bring someone flowers?
    _____

11. When did you last do the dishes?
    _____

12. When did you last find a penny on the sidewalk?
    _____

13. When did you last send a telegram?
    _____

14. When did you last go to a wedding?
    _____

SHE ATTENDED HIGH SCHOOL FOR FOUR YEARS.

Affirmative Statements

Regular and Irregular Past Tense Verbs

APPLICATION FOR EMPLOYMENT

Name _Linda Lee_

Address _49 Laguna Street_

Laguna Beach, California

Telephone Number _(555) 984-6621_

EDUCATION

Name of School	Major Subject	Dates Attended	Grades Completed	Degree Received
Huntington Elementary School	——	1960 – 1968	1st – 8th	——
Newport High School	——	1969 – 1973	9th – 12th	diploma
The University of California	English	1974 – 1978	——	bachelor's degree

New Words: degree = an award for achievement in a college or university

major subject = the chief course of study a person takes when completing a degree (such as history or English)

grade = a particular year of a school course (second grade, tenth grade)

1969-1973 = from 1969 to 1973

Note: In the United States, students attend elementary school and junior high school for eight years. Then they attend high school for four years. When they graduate, they receive a diploma. Some students go to a college or a university. If they go to college (usually for four years) and graduate, they receive a bachelor's degree.

SHE ATTENDED HIGH SCHOOL FOR FOUR YEARS.

When did she attend high school?   She attended high school from 1969 to 1973.
What high school did she go to?   She went to Newport High School.

PRACTICE

Look at the application on page 20. Then answer the questions in complete sentences.

1. What elementary school did Linda Lee go to?
   She went to Huntington Elementary School.

2. When did she attend Huntington Elementary School?
   _____

3. How long did she attend Huntington Elementary School?
   _____

4. What was the last grade she completed?
   _____

5. How long did she attend high school?
   _____

6. What high school did she go to?
   _____

7. When did she attend Newport High School?
   _____

8. What was the last grade she completed?
   _____

9. What degree did she receive?
   _____

10. What high school did she graduate from?
    _____

11. What college did she go to?
    _____

12. What was her major subject?
    _____

13. When did she attend the University of California?
    _____

14. What degree did she receive?
    _____

HE SOLD FURNITURE.

Affirmative Statements
Regular and Irregular Past Tense Verbs

What was his position at Ames Department Store? He `was` a sales clerk.

What did he do at Ames Department Store?   He `sold` furniture.

Note: irregular past tense verbs:

teach → taught   leave → left   get → got   sell → sold

APPLICATION FOR EMPLOYMENT

Name   _Harry Smith_
Address   _4224 Maple Avenue_
              Oakland, California

Telephone Number _(715) 555-1660_

Work Experience (most recent listed first)

Company	Position	Work You Did	Dates Worked	Yearly Salary	Reason for Leaving
Greenfield High School	English teacher	Taught English	1981 - 1992	$27,500	Got a job in California
Ames Department Store	Sales clerk	Sold furniture	1978 - 1980	$10,400	Got a job teaching in Massachusetts

HE SOLD FURNITURE.

PRACTICE

Look at the application on page 22. Then answer the questions in complete sentences.

1. Where did Harry Smith work from 1981 to 1992?

   He worked at Greenfield High School.

2. What was his position?

   _____

3. What did he do?

   _____

4. How long did he work for Greenfield High School?

   _____

5. How much did he earn?

   _____

6. Why did he leave Greenfield High School?

   _____

7. Where did he work from 1978 to 1980?

   _____

8. What was his position?

   _____

9. What did he do?

   _____

10. How long did he work for Ames Department Store?

    _____

11. How much did he earn?

    _____

12. Why did he leave Ames Department Store?

    _____

MAKE IT WORK

Answer the questions about your first job.

Where did you work? _____

What did you do? _____

WHY DID YOU LEAVE AMES DEPARTMENT STORE?

Questions with _When, How, Why, What, Who, Where_

Regular and Irregular Past Tense Verbs

> I   left   Ames Department Store.
>
> **Why** did you **leave** Ames Department Store?

PRACTICE

Make questions.

I worked for Star Shoe Company.

1. When _did you work for Star Shoe Company?_ _____

2. How long _____

3. Who _____ for?

She left A. B. C. Company.

4. When _____

5. Why _____

I graduated from college.

6. When _____

7. What college _____ from?

He attended high school.

8. Where _____

9. When _____

10. What high school _____

She worked for National Bank.

11. How long _____

12. Who _____ for?

He earned a lot of money at Selby Company.

13. How much _____

I taught at Harbor High School.

14. What _____

15. When _____

16. How long _____

SHE SERVED HER FAMILY TURKEY.

Indirect Objects

Regular and Irregular Past Tense Verbs

	objects	
	indirect	**direct**
She served		turkey.
She served	her family	turkey.

Note: You can place the indirect object before the direct object.

PRACTICE

Add the indirect objects to the sentences.

1. Barbara Ann sent holiday cards. (her friends)

   Barbara Ann sent her friends holiday cards.

2. She mailed a gift. (her grandmother)

   _____

3. She bought a blouse. (her mother)

   _____

4. She got toys. (her children)

   _____

5. She gave a book. (her father)

   _____

6. She made an apron. (her sister)

   _____

7. She baked cookies. (her aunt and uncle)

   _____

8. She got a tie. (her husband)

   _____

9. She cooked a big meal. (her family)

   _____

10. She served turkey. (everyone)

    _____

MAKE IT WORK

Tell who you gave gifts to last holiday season and tell what you gave each person.

I gave my father a tie.

_____

_____

THE WAITER HANDED MENUS TO THEM.

Indirect Objects

Regular and Irregular Past Tense Verbs

	objects	
	indirect **direct**	**indirect**
The waiter handed	them menus.	
The waiter handed	menus	to them.

Note: You can place the indirect object after the direct object if you use *to* or *for* before the indirect object.

Use *to* after these verbs: Use *for* after these verbs:
bring   give   serve   hand   find   pour   order   leave

PRACTICE

Rewrite the sentences by placing the indirect object after the direct object.

1. The hostess finally found them a table.

   The hostess finally found a table for them.

2. The waiter brought them some wine.

   _____

3. He poured Mr. Green and Mr. Bang some wine.

   _____

4. Then the waiter handed them menus.

   _____

5. Mr. Green gave the waiter their order.

   _____

6. He ordered them steak.

   _____

7. After fifteen minutes the waiter served them their food.

   _____

8. When the meal was over, the waiter handed Mr. Green the check.

   _____

9. Mr. Green gave the waiter some money.

   _____

10. He also left the waiter a tip.

    _____

New Word: tip = a small payment for service, usually 15% of the check

HE LEFT A TIP FOR THE WAITER.

To, For, or No Preposition with Indirect Objects

Regular and Irregular Past Tense Verbs

	indirect	**objects** direct	indirect
He left the	waiter	a tip.	
He left		a tip	[for] the waiter.

Note: Use *to* or *for* when the indirect object comes after the direct object.
Do not use *to* or *for* when the indirect object comes first.

PRACTICE

Fill in the blanks with *to, for,* or a line (—) for nothing.

1. The hostess finally found _____—_____ them a table.

2. The hostess finally found a table _____*for*_____ them.

3. The waiter brought some wine _____ them.

4. He poured _____ Mr. Green some wine.

5. He also poured some wine _____ Mr. Bang.

6. The waiter handed _____ Mr. Green a menu.

7. Then he handed a menu _____ Mr. Bang.

8. After Mr. Green and Mr. Bang looked at the menus, Mr. Green gave their order _____ the waiter.

9. He ordered steak _____ both of them.

10. After fifteen minutes, the waiter brought _____ them their food.

11. After dinner, the waiter served dessert _____ them.

12. When the meal was over, the waiter handed the check _____ Mr. Green.

13. Mr. Green gave _____ the waiter some money.

14. Mr. Green also left a tip _____ the waiter.

THEY CAUGHT THE THIEF.

Review: Simple Past

| begin → began | come → came | hit → hit | run → ran |

PRACTICE

There are many stories about people who call for help and nobody comes. Here's a story about a person who called for help and everybody came. Fill in the blanks with the correct past form.

Phyllis North, age 45, _____*had*_____ her purse taken from her on a
(1. have)

street in Chicago. She _____, and then she
(2. scream)

_____ to chase the thief. Michael Maloney, age 24, was driving
(3. start)

his car down the street when he_____ a man running and a
(4. see)

woman running after him. Maloney _____ the man with his car.
(5. chase)

When the man _____ between two buildings, Maloney
(6. run)

_____ one of the buildings.
(7. hit)

Several people _____ to see what the noise was. When they
(8. come)

_____ about the thief, they _____ to chase him
(9. hear)   (10. begin)

too. Other people _____ the chase along the way. Finally
(11. join)

Maloney and another man _____ the thief and
(12. catch)

_____ the purse. Several other people _____
(13. find)   (14. hear)

Phyllis North scream, and they all _____ the police.
(15. call)

"It was beautiful," said Maloney. "At least fifty people tried to catch the

thief."

New Word: join = take part in

I REFUSE TO GIVE UP THIS DREAM.

Verb + Gerund vs. Verb + Infinitive

Simple Present, Future with _Will_

	verb	gerund	verb	infinitive	
I'd like to	quit	working	, but I need	to support	my family.

Note: Use the gerund form after these verbs:

finish	imagine	consider	mind	practice
keep (on)	miss	enjoy	quit	

Use the infinitive form after these verbs:

want	hope	need	have
expect	plan	refuse	would like

PRACTICE

Read what these people say about their hopes and dreams. Fill in the blanks with a gerund or an infinitive.

I hope _____*to be*_____ a concert

(1. to be)

pianist. I practice _____ the piano

(2. play)

about five hours a day. When I finish

_____, I listen to music. My

(3. practice)

whole life is music. I can't imagine

_____ anything else. Some day,

(4. do)

if I keep on _____, I'll be a great

(5. practice)

pianist. I refuse _____ up this

(6. give)

dream.

Curtis Jones, age 12

New Words: keep on = continue

refuse = agree not to do something

imagine = picture in one's mind

I REFUSE TO GIVE UP THIS DREAM.

I'm a high school student. My boyfriend and

I are considering _____
(7. get)

married after we graduate. We plan

_____ children right away. I
(8. have)

want _____ a lot of children
(9. have)

—maybe four or five. I think I'll enjoy

_____ at home and
(10. stay)

Alice Anderson, age 17   _____ a mother. And I'd like
(11. be)

_____ a house. I don't expect _____ one
(12. own)   (13. buy)

right away, but that's my dream.

I'm a truck driver. I don't mind

_____ trucks, but I'm on the road
(14. drive)

for two weeks at a time, and I miss

_____ my family. I'd like to quit
(15. see)

_____, but I need
(16. work)

_____ my family. My dream is to
(17. support)

get a job closer to home so I don't have

_____ away so much.
(18. be)

John Murphy, age 40

New Words: mind = be troubled by
consider = think about carefully
support = pay expenses for the cost of living

30

THEY DECIDED TO RETIRE.

Verb + Gerund vs. Verb + Infinitive

Present, Past, Future with *Will*

> They decided | to retire. | They appreciate | having | more free time.
> Note: Use the infinitive form   Note: Use the gerund form after the
>   after the verb *decide*.   the verb *appreciate*.

PRACTICE

Fill in the blanks with a gerund or an infinitve.

1. (retire) When Kay and Jack were 65 years old, they decided
   _____*to retire*_____.

2. (have) At first they expected _____ nothing to do all day.

3. (retire) "I can't imagine _____," said Jack. "My job is my
   whole life."

4. (work/do) Kay kept on _____ for a few months after Jack
   retired because she said she needed _____ something.

5. (be) Today they don't mind _____ at home.

6. (work) In fact they don't miss _____ at all.

7. (swim/garden) Jack and Kay enjoy _____ and
   _____.

8. (do) They appreciate _____ things they never had time to
   do before.

9. (write/take) Jack is considering_____ a book in the
   future, and Kay wants _____ some cooking classes.

10. (travel) Next year they also hope _____ to Venezuela.

MAKE IT WORK

Fill in the blanks.

When I retire, I hope _____. I want _____

_____. I won't miss _____

_____. I'll enjoy _____

_____.

New Word: retire = give up a job and stop working, often because of age

IN MY FREE TIME, I LIKE TO GO SHOPPING.

Go + Gerund, Verb + Gerund, Verb + Infinitive

Simple Present, Simple Past

>   **gerund**
>
> In my free time, I like to go | shopping. |
>
>   I also   like to go | swimming. |
>
> Note: *Go* is followed by a gerund with these verbs:
>
> | | | | |
> |---|---|---|---|
> | shop | swim | camp | dance |
> | jog | ski | hike | fish |
>
> Use the infinitive after the verbs *learn* and *afford*.
> Use the gerund after the verb *dislike*.
> You can use the infinitive or gerund after the verb *like*.

PRACTICE

Read what these people like to do in their free time. Fill in the blanks with a gerund or an infinitive.

Samantha Porter, age 30

In my free time, I like to go

_____*shopping*_____. I can't afford
(1.shop)

_____ everything I see, but I
(2. buy)

like _____.
(3. look)

I enjoy _____. I go
(4. dance)

_____ every Saturday night.
(5. dance)

I'm learning _____ the tango,
(6 dance)

and I love it. Next, I want

_____ to line dance.
(7. learn)

Jane Lucks, age 71

IN MY FREE TIME, I LIKE TO GO SHOPPING.

I quit _____ last year. Now
(8. smoke)

I'm into health and exercise. I go

_____ a lot, and I also go
(9. jog)

_____ at a health club.
(10. swim)

Ken Fan, age 25

I enjoy _____ outdoors. I go
(11. be)

_____ several times a year. I also
(12. fish)

go _____ once a year. My wife
(13. camp)

dislikes _____ and
(14. fish)

_____, and she refuses
(15. camp)

_____ with me. So I go with the
(16. go)

guys at work.

Jimmy Blackhawk, age 46

MAKE IT WORK

Tell what you enjoy doing in your free time.

_____

_____

_____

New Words: line dance = dance in a line with other people
be into = be interested in
afford = be able to pay for something

SHE ENJOYS WORKING. SHE WANTS TO WORK.

Review: Verb + Gerund vs. Verb + Infinitive

Present, Future with *Going To*

	verb	gerund		verb	infinitive	
	She enjoys	working.		She wants	to work	as long as possible.

PRACTICE

Fill in the blanks with a gerund or an infinitive.

1. (work) Laura is expecting a baby. She wants _____*to work*_____ until the baby arrives.

2. (take) Then she expects _____ a leave of absence.

3. (work) She's going to quit _____ at the end of the month.

4. (go) After she has the baby, she'd like _____ back to work in a month.

5. (work) She's going to be a mother, and she's going to keep on _____ at the same time.

6. (work) She doesn't need _____, but she wants to.

7. (work) She enjoys _____.

8. (be) She also wants _____ a mother.

9. (have) It's going to be hard, but she doesn't mind _____ two jobs.

10. (give) She refuses _____ up her career as a teacher.

11. (stay) Besides, she can't imagine _____ at home all the time.

12. (be) She hopes _____ a good teacher and a good mother.

MAKE IT WORK

Complete the sentences about yourself.

I want _____.

I need _____.

I need to quit _____.

New Word: leave of absence = permission to be absent from work, usually for a long period of time

34

SHE MADE A MISTAKE.

Make vs. *Do*

Simple Past

She did	her homework.	She made	a mistake.
	an exercise.		an error.
	an assignment.		breakfast.
	the housework.		dinner.
	the dishes.		the beds.
	the laundry.		an appointment.
	the ironing.		a telephone call.
She didn't do	her best.		
	a good job.		

PRACTICE

Fill in the blanks with the correct form of *make* or *do*.

Bernadette got up early yesterday. It was a very busy day. First she

_____made_____ the beds. Then she _____ breakfast for her family
    (1)   (2)

and _____ the dishes. After everyone was gone, she _____
       (3)   (4)

some housework. She washed the kitchen floor, and she dusted. She also

_____ the laundry, and then she _____ some ironing.
   (5)   (6)

After lunch, she _____ a telephone call. She called her French
                    (7)

tutor. She _____ an appointment for 4:00 instead of 3:00. Then she
         (8)

quickly _____ her homework. She had to _____ five
       (9)   (10)

exercises. She _____ her best to finish, but she only _____
         (11)   (12)

four exercises. She knew that she didn't _____ a good job. She knew
                              (13)

that she _____ some mistakes because she _____ her
      (14)   (15)

assignment in a hurry. Then she got into her car and drove to her tutor's house.

New Word: tutor = private teacher

35

MY HUSBAND DOES THE ERRANDS.

Make vs. *Do*

Simple Present

My husband does the errands.   I make dinner.

Note: Use *do* with these words: Note: Use *make* with these words:
yardwork   plans
shopping   reservations
errands   arrangements
correspondence

PRACTICE

Below is a list of chores. Tell who does each chore in your family. Use *make* or *do* and the present tense.

1. the laundry   *I do the laundry.*

2. dinner   _____

3. the dinner dishes   _____

4. the food shopping   _____

5. doctor appointments   _____

6. the housework   _____

7. plans to see friends   _____

8. the correspondence   _____

9. travel arrangements   _____

10. the errands   _____

11. restaurant reservations   _____

12. the yardwork   _____

MAKE IT WORK

Name two chores you like to do.

I like to do the food shopping. _____

_____

_____

New Word: correspondence = the writing and exchanging of letters

I'LL PROBABLY GO SHOPPING THIS WEEKEND.

Affirmative Statements

Future with *Will*

I	**'ll probably go**	to the movies this weekend.
I	**'ll do**	my homework.

PRACTICE

Look at the chart below. Then tell some things you'll do this weekend.

I'll probably	clean my room. go to the movies. take a drive. read a book. do some yardwork. go shopping. visit my friends. write some letters. go out for dinner.	do my homework. do the laundry. go to a party. rent a video. watch TV. go to church. sleep late. play cards. call my family.

1. *I'll probably go shopping this weekend.* _____
2. _____
3. _____
4. _____
5. _____
6. _____
7. _____
8. _____
9. _____
10. _____
11. _____
12. _____
13. _____
14. _____

WHEN MY SISTER GETS MARRIED, SHE'LL HAVE A BIG WEDDING.

Affirmative Statements with *After, Before,* **and** *When*

Future with *Will*

> When my sister gets married next month, she 'll have a big wedding.
>
> My sister will have a big wedding when she gets married next month.
>
> Note: To express a future idea, use the present tense in clauses beginning with *after, before,* or *when.* Use the future tense in the main clause.

PRACTICE

Read each sentence first. Then fill in the blanks with the correct verb tense.

1. When my sister (get) _____ *gets* _____ married next month, she and her husband (have) _____ *will have* _____ a big wedding.

2. Diane (look) _____ beautiful when she (walk) _____ down the aisle.

3. After the ceremony (be) _____ over, she and her husband (leave) _____ the church.

4. A photographer (take) _____ their picture before they (leave) _____ the church.

5. When they (leave) _____ the church, everyone (throw) _____ rice.

6. After Diane and her husband (arrive) _____ at the reception, everyone (drink) _____ champagne.

7. After Diane and her husband (dance) _____, everyone (dance) _____.

8. Diane (throw)_____ a bouquet of flowers before she and her husband (leave) _____ the reception.

9. The person who catches the bouquet (be) _____ the next person to get married.

10. After Diane (throw) _____ the bouquet, she and her husband (get) _____ into a car and drive away.

AFTER YUKIKO LEAVES TOKYO, SHE'LL GO TO LONDON.

Affirmative Statements with *After* and *When*

Furture with *Will*

> First Yukiko will leave Tokyo. Then she'll go to London.
>
> After Yukiko | leaves | Tokyo, she | 'll go | to London.
>
> Note: Use the present tense in clauses beginning with *when* or *after*.
> Use the future tense in the main clause. Put a comma (,) after the
> *when* or *after* clause if it comes first in the sentence.

PRACTICE

Combine the sentences with *after* or *when*. Use contractions if possible.

1. First Yukiko will leave Tokyo. Then she'll go to London.

   After *Yukiko leaves Tokyo, she'll go to London.*

2. She'll see London. After that she'll fly to Paris.

   After _____

3. She'll be in Paris. At that time she'll see the Eiffel Tower.

   When _____

4. She'll leave Paris. Then she'll go to Rome.

   After _____

5. She'll visit Rome. She'll go to some museums.

   When _____

6. She'll be in Rome. She'll see some famous fountains.

   When _____

7. She'll see Rome. Afterwards she'll go to Madrid.

   After _____

8. She'll spend a day in Madrid. Then she'll go to Athens.

   After _____

9. She'll visit Athens. She'll see some famous statues.

   When _____

10. She'll leave Athens. She'll fly back to Tokyo.

    After _____

New Words: fountain    statue

IF IT RAINS THIS WEEKEND, I'LL STAY AT HOME.

Negative and Affirmative Statements

Future Real Conditional

If it [rains] this weekend, I ['ll stay] at home.

I [won't go] to the beach.

Note: The future conditional is used to express a situation that is
expected as a result of some condition.
Use the present tense in the *if*-clause; use the future tense in the
main clause.

PRACTICE

Look at the chart below. Then tell some things you'll do this weekend. Begin
your sentences with *If*.

			stay at home. work in the yard. wash the car. go to the beach. go swimming. play golf. take a walk. water the plants. mow the lawn. go fishing.
If it rains If it's sunny	this weekend,	I'll I won't	

1. <u>If it rains this weekend, I won't work in the yard.</u>

2. _____

3. _____

4. _____

5. _____

6. _____

7. _____

8. _____

9. _____

10. _____

I'D TAKE A KNIFE WITH ME ON THE LIFEBOAT.

Negative and Affirmative Statements

Present Unreal Conditional

If you were shipwrecked, what
would you take with you on the lifeboat?

I ⌜'d take⌝ a knife with me.

I ⌜wouldn't take⌝ any money.

Note: Use the present unreal conditional
for imaginary situations.

contractions: I'd = I would   wouldn't = would not

PRACTICE

Tell which things you would take with you on the lifeboat and which things
you wouldn't take. Use contractions.

1. some money _____I wouldn't take any money with me._____

2. some matches _____

3. a pen _____

4. some paper _____

5. an umbrella _____

6. a knife _____

7. a candy bar _____

8. a blanket _____

9. a can opener _____

10. a flashlight _____

11. a radio _____

12. a book _____

13. some water _____

14. a can of tuna _____

MAKE IT WORK

If you were allowed to take only two things on the lifeboat, which things
would they be? Why?

I'd take _____

_____

IF I WERE A MOVIE STAR, I'D MAKE A LOT OF MONEY.

Affirmative Statements with _Were_

Present Unreal Conditional

> If I [were] a movie star, I ['d make] a lot of money.

Note: Use _if_ + _were_ and _would_ + the simple form of the verb for unreal
possibilities in the present.
Use _were_ for all persons.

PRACTICE

First answer each question with _yes_ or _no_. Then make sentences for every
question you answered with _no_.

1. Are you a movie star?   _No_

   If I were a movie star, I'd make a cowboy movie.

2. Are you an artist?   _____

   _____

3. Are you a doctor?   _____

   _____

4. Are you a corporation president?   _____

   _____

   _____

5. Are you a pilot?   _____

   _____

6. Are you a photographer?   _____

   _____

7. Are you a secretary?   _____

   _____

8. Are you a pianist?   _____

   _____

9. Are you a novelist?   _____

   _____

10. Are you a gardener?   _____

   _____

IF I SAW AN ACCIDENT, I'D CALL AN AMBULANCE.

Affirmative Statements

Present Unreal Conditional

> If I ⟨saw⟩ an accident, I ⟨'d call⟩ an ambulance.
>
> Note: Use the past tense with *if*-clauses.
>
> irregular past tense verbs: break → broke   lose → lost
>
> feel → felt   steal → stole

PRACTICE

Answer the questions in complete sentences. Use contractions if possible.

1. Who would you call if you had a personal problem?

   If I had a personal problem, I'd call my mother.

2. Who would you call if you needed money?

   _____

3. What would you do if you had a headache?

   _____

4. What would you do if you felt sick?

   _____

5. Who would you call if you broke your arm?

   _____

6. Who would you call if your house were on fire?

   _____

7. Who would you call if you saw a car accident?

   _____

8. Who would you call if someone robbed your house or apartment?

   _____

9. What would you do if you lost the keys to your house or apartment?

   _____

10. Who would you call if someone stole your wallet?

   _____

MAKE IT WORK

Fill in the blanks with emergency telephone numbers in your area.

Ambulance _____

Police _____

Fire _____

43

IF I INHERITED SOME MONEY, I'D TAKE A TRIP AROUND THE WORLD.

Review: Present Unreal and Future Real Conditionals

real condition:	If I take a vacation for two weeks, I 'll go to Maine.
unreal condition:	If I took a vacation for two months, I 'd go to Egypt.

PRACTICE

Put a check next to all the activities that will probably happen to you in the near future. Then make sentences with *if* for all of the phrases.

1. ✓ take a vacation for two weeks

   If I take a vacation for two weeks, I'll go to Maine.

2. _____ take a vacation for two months

   If I took a vacation for two months, I'd go to Egypt.

3. _____ buy a new car

   _____

4. _____ own a sailboat

   _____

5. _____ move

   _____

6. _____ be famous

   _____

7. _____ buy a new television

   _____

8. _____ buy a computer

   _____

9. _____ inherit some money

   _____

10. _____ go back to school

    _____

11. _____ save some money

    _____

12. _____ lose weight

    _____

THEY'RE WORKING FOR THEIR FATHER NOW.

Affirmative and Negative Statements
Present Continuous

Tina	is teaching	now.
Dave and his brother	are working	for their father now.
Patty	isn't working	now.
Bill and his wife	aren't working	now.

teach → teach ing   write → writ ing   forget → forget ting

work → work ing   live → liv ing   sit → sit ting

Note: Add *ing* to the simple form of the verb.

If a verb ends in consonant + *e*, omit the *e* and add *ing*.

If a verb ends in consonant + vowel + consonant, double the last consonant before adding *ing*.

PRACTICE

Tina meets Bev in a department store, and they talk about what their high school friends are doing. Fill in the blanks with the correct form of the present continuous. Use contractions with pronouns.

Bev: Tina Palaferri!

Tina: Bev Smith. I can't believe it! How are you?

Bev: I'm fine. I __'m working__ in a bank now. What are you doing?
(1. work)

Tina: I _____ now.
(2. teach)

Bev: How about LuEllen? What's she doing?

Tina: I'm not sure. I think she _____ to school.
(3. go)

Bev: Do you remember Mary Ann?

Tina: Yes, of course.

Bev: Her husband _____ a novel.
(4. write)

Tina: What about Patty?

Bev: She _____. She and her husband
(5. not/work)

_____ a new house in Laguna Beach.
(6. build)

THEY'RE WORKING FOR THEIR FATHER NOW.

Tina: How are Dave Robertson and his brother Mike?

Bev: They _____ very well. They _____ for
               (7. do)   (8. work)

their father now. What's Rich Elliott doing?

Tina: He _____ at Princeton University.
            (9. study)

He _____ a law degree.
      (10. get)

Bev: I think Inez Naples _____ to Princeton too. How are Sue
                              (11. go)

and Tom Corkett?

Tina: They_____ in Texas now. They _____ for
             (12. live)   (13. work)

a real estate company. Tom _____ houses, and Sue
                                  (14. build)

_____ them.
      (15. sell)

Bev: What's Tom's brother Bill doing?

Tina: He and his wife _____ in New York. They
                           (16. live)

_____ very well. Bill _____ now, and his
      (17. not/do)   (18. not/work)

wife _____ for a job. I think
          (19. look)

they _____ a divorce.
          (20. get)

Bev: I'm sorry to hear that. Well, I have to go now. It's great to see you.

Tina: Good to see you too. Bye.

MAKE IT WORK

Tell about two of your school friends.

_____

_____

New Words: real estate company = a business that sells land and houses
                   divorce = the ending of a marriage by a court

46

HE'S CHANGING PLANES IN CHICAGO.

Present Continuous with Future Intention

He | **'s changing** | planes in Chicago.

Note: You can use the present continuous to express future time when talking about definite plans, like schedules.

PRACTICE

John Burns is going to take a trip to New York. Tell about his schedule. Use the present continuous.

1. Leave Seattle on June 28th.

   He's leaving Seattle on June 28th.

2. Fly on American Airlines.

   _____

3. Stop in Chicago for an hour.

   _____

4. Change planes in Chicago.

   _____

5. Fly to New York on United Airlines.

   _____

6. Arrive in New York at 6:38 P.M.

   _____

7. Stay in New York for three days.

   _____

8. Return to Seattle on July 2nd.

   _____

9. Leave at 12:50 P.M.

   _____

10. Fly directly to Seattle.

    _____

11. Fly on TWA.

    _____

12. Arrive in Seattle at 9:20 P.M.

    _____

THE CHILDREN DOWN THE STREET WERE PLAYING TENNIS.

Affirmative Statements

Past Continuous

> A woman on Maple Avenue | was cleaning | her house.
> The children down the street | were playing | tennis.
>
> Note: Use *was* or *were* + verb + *ing* to form the past continuous.

PRACTICE

Fill in the blanks with the past continuous.

There was a car accident on the corner of Fifth Street and Maple Avenue at 9:30 A.M. yesterday. No one saw the accident. Tell what each person was doing at 9:30 yesterday.

1. (talk) A man on Fifth Street and Maple Avenue *was talking* on the telephone.

2. (make) A woman on Fifth Street _____ breakfast.

3. (clean) A woman on Maple Avenue _____ her house.

4. (jog) A man and a woman on Fifth Street _____ in the park.

5. (play) The children down the street _____ tennis.

6. (work) A man on Fifth Street _____ in his back yard.

7. (sleep) A man and his son on Maple Avenue _____.

8. (listen) A girl on Fourth Street _____ to the radio.

9. (study) Two teenage boys in the next block _____ at the library.

10. (watch) The babysitter on the next corner _____ the children.

11. (exercise) A man and a woman on Maple Avenue _____ at a health club.

12. (take) The woman in the yellow house on Maple Avenue _____ a bath.

13. (eat) A man and a woman on Fifth Street _____ breakfast.

14. (use) The man on the corner of Maple Avenue and Fourth Street _____ his computer.

48

HE WAS STUDYING WHEN THE DOORBELL RANG.

Affirmative Statements with *When*

Past Continuous

> He was studying from 9:00 to 10:00. The doorbell rang at 10:00.
>
> He │ was studying │ when the doorbell │ rang. │
>
> Note: Use the past tense with an action that interrupts a longer, continuing action.
>
> continuing action: He was studying.
> interrupting action: The doorbell rang.
>
> irregular verbs: ring → rang   eat → ate
> (For other irregular past tense verbs, see pages 19 and 28.)

PRACTICE

Combine the sentences with *when*.

1. He read the newspaper. The telephone rang.

   He was reading the newspaper when the telephone rang.

2. He talked on the telephone. The accident happened.

   _____

3. He watched television. Steve came over.

   _____

4. He relaxed on the patio. It began to rain.

   _____

5. He cooked dinner. The baby started to cry.

   _____

6. He ate dinner. He heard a loud noise.

   _____

7. He studied. The doorbell rang.

   _____

8. He took a bath. Mary called.

   _____

9. He read a book. The dog started to bark.

   _____

10. He took a nap. His alarm clock went off.

   _____

SHE HURT HER BACK WHILE SHE WAS MOVING FURNITURE.

Affirmative Statements with *While*

Past Continuous

> She hurt her back.   She was moving furniture.
>
> She | hurt | her back while she | was moving | furniture.
>
> Note: Use the past continuous with a longer, continuing action.
>   Use the past tense with the action that interrupts the continuing action.
>
> irregular past tense verbs: break → broke   fall → fell   tear → tore
>   cut → cut   hurt → hurt

P R A C T I C E

Answer the questions with *while*.

1. When did he cut his face? (shave)

   He cut his face while he was shaving.

2. When did she hurt her back? (move furniture)

   _____

3. When did he cut his finger? (cook)

   _____

4. When did you fall down? (I/ride a bicycle)

   _____

5. When did he slip? (walk in the snow)

   _____

6. When did she bump her head? (get out of the car)

   _____

7. When did he tear his pants? (work in the yard)

   _____

8. When did you burn your hand? (I/cook)

   _____

9. When did they have an accident? (drive)

   _____

10. When did he break his leg? (play football)

    _____

HE BROKE A GLASS WHILE HE WAS DOING THE DISHES.

Affirmative Statements with *When* and *While*

Past Continuous

He broke a glass while he was doing the dishes.
While he was doing the dishes, he broke a glass.

He was making breakfast when the telephone rang.
When the telephone rang, he was making breakfast.

Note: Use the past continuous with a longer continuing action; use the past tense with a short, interrupting action.

PRACTICE

Fill in the blanks with the correct verb tense. Be sure to read each sentence first.

1. Joe (sleep) _____*was sleeping*_____ when his alarm clock accidentally
   (go) _____*went*_____ off at 7:00 last Saturday morning.

2. He (cut) _____ his face while he (shave)
   _____.

3. While he (take) _____ a shower, the telephone (ring)
   _____.

4. He (take) _____ a shower when he (slip)
   _____ and (fall) _____.

5. The telephone (ring) _____ again while he (make)
   _____ breakfast.

6. While he (talk) _____ on the telephone, the toast
   (begin) _____ to burn.

7. He (make) _____ the coffee when he (knock)
   _____ over the coffee pot.

8. While he (fry) _____ some eggs, he (burn)
   _____ his hand.

9. Then he (break) _____ a glass while he (do)
   _____ the dishes.

10. He (decide) _____ it was a bad day, so he (go)
    _____ back to bed.

THE MAN IN THE LOBBY HAS BEEN WAITING SINCE 1:20.

Affirmative Statements

Present Perfect Continuous

THE MAN IN THE LOBBY HAS BEEN WAITING SINCE 1:20.

He ｜'s been filing｜ since 12:30.   They ｜'ve been filing｜ since 12:30.

Note: Use the present perfect continuous for an action that began in the past and continues up to the present. Use the continuous of the present perfect for activities that are in progress at the moment of speaking.

Form the present perfect continuous with *have* or *has* + *been* + verb + *ing*.

contractions: he's = he has   they've = they have

PRACTICE

Look at page 52. Then answer the questions with *since*. Use contractions whenever possible.

1. How long have the clerks been filing?

   They've been filing since 12:30.

2. How long have the typists been typing?

   _____

3. How long has the assistant manager been looking at the bulletin board?

   _____

   _____

4. How long has the office manager been talking on the telephone?

   _____

5. How long have the accountants been checking figures?

   _____

6. How long has the receptionist been sitting at the switchboard?

   _____

7. How long has the man in the lobby been waiting?

   _____

8. How long has the boss's secretary been opening the mail?

   _____

9. How long has the salesperson been writing a report?

   _____

10. How long has the boss been out to lunch?

   _____

HAS HE BEEN WAITING SINCE 1:20? YES, HE HAS.

Negative and Affirmative Short Answers

Present Perfect Continuous

> Has the man been waiting since 1:45?
> Has he been waiting since 1:20?
> Have the typists been typing since 10:00?
> Have they been typing since 12:00?
>
> | No, he hasn't. |
> | Yes, he has. |
> | No, they haven't. |
> | Yes, they have. |
>
> contractions: hasn't = has not   haven't = have not

PRACTICE

Look at the picture on page 52. Then answer the questions with short answers.

1. Has the boss been out to lunch since 1:00? <u>No, he hasn't.</u>

2. Has he been out to lunch since 11:30? <u>Yes, he has.</u>

3. Have the typists been typing since 10:00? _____

4. Have they been typing since 12:00? _____

5. Has the office manager been talking on the telephone since 1:30? _____

6. Have the clerks been filing since 11:30? _____

7. Have they been filing since 12:30? _____

8. Have the accountants been checking figures since 9:00? _____

9. Have they been checking figures since 12:00? _____

10. Has the man in the lobby been waiting since 1:45? _____

11. Has he been waiting since 1:20? _____

12. Has the boss's secretary been opening the mail since 12:45? _____

13. Has she been opening the mail since 1:45? _____

14. Has the salesperson been writing a report since 9:00? _____

15. Has he been writing a report since 11:00? _____

HOW LONG HAS SHE BEEN TYPING THE REPORT?

Questions with *How Long*

Present Perfect Continuous

She 's been typing the report.

How long | has she been typing the report?

PRACTICE

Make questions with *how long*.

1. They've been using the adding machines.

   How long have they been using the adding machines?

2. We've been listening to the boss.

   _____

3. I've been working on the report.

   _____

4. He's been talking on the telephone.

   _____

5. They've been eating lunch.

   _____

6. She's been sitting at the switchboard.

   _____

7. I've been waiting in the lobby.

   _____

8. He's been using the computer.

   _____

9. We've been filing letters.

   _____

10. They've been reading the mail.

    _____

11. She's been standing at the coffee machine.

    _____

12. I've been typing letters.

    _____

SHE'S WASHED THE CLOTHES ONCE SO FAR.

Affirmative Statements

Present Perfect: Regular Past Participles

WEEKLY CHORES

		M	T	W	Th	F	S
Myra	wash the clothes	✔					
	cook dinner	✔	✔		✔		
	vacuum		✔				
	iron the clothes				✔		
Myra and Becky	change the beds	✔					
Roy	clean his room		✔				
	water the plants	✔			✔		
	empty the waste paper baskets		✔				
Becky	dust the living room			✔			
	clean her room		✔				
Roy and Becky	clean the bathroom			✔			
	wash the dishes	✔	✔	✔	✔		
Bill	cook dinner			✔			
	carry out the trash				✔		

I	**'ve washed**	the clothes once this week.
She	's	
He	's	
They	've	

Note: Use the present perfect for an action that began in the past and continues up to the present.

The present perfect is formed with *have/has* + the past participle. Regular past participles are formed by adding *d* or *ed* to the simple form of the verb.

change → change d   clean → clean ed

contractions: she's = she has   I've = I have

SHE'S WASHED THE CLOTHES ONCE SO FAR.

PRACTICE

Look at page 56. Then tell what chores each person has done so far this week. Write sentences with the present perfect tense. Use contractions whenever possible.

1. _Myra has washed the clothes once so far._
2. _____
3. _____
4. _____
5. _____
6. _____
7. _____
8. _____

_____

9. _____
10. _____
11. _____
12. _____
13. _____
14. _____

MAKE IT WORK

Name three chores you've done this week.

I've washed the kithen floor.

_____

_____

_____

New Words: once = one time
twice = two times

SHE HASN'T WATERED THE PLANTS FOR TWO DAYS.

Since and *For*

Present Perfect

> She hasn't changed the beds | for | two days.
>
> She hasn't changed the beds | since | Monday.
>
> Note: Use *for* with a period of time.
>
> Monday → Tuesday → Wednesday for two days
>
> Use *since* with a beginning time.
>
> Monday Tuesday Wednesday   since Monday

PRACTICE

Fill in the blanks with *since* or *for*.

1. She hasn't washed the dishes _____*for*_____ a week.

2. She hasn't washed the dishes _____*since*_____ Monday.

3. She hasn't vacuumed the floors _____ a month.

4. She hasn't polished the furniture _____ March.

5. She hasn't changed the beds _____ two weeks.

6. She hasn't dusted the bookshelves _____ Tuesday.

7. She hasn't washed the windows _____ May.

8. She hasn't cleaned the oven _____ two months.

9. She hasn't defrosted the refrigerator _____ last summer.

10. She hasn't waxed the kitchen floor _____ three months.

11. She hasn't watered the plants _____ a week.

12. She hasn't cleaned the bathroom _____ Saturday.

13. She hasn't taken out the trash _____ yesterday.

14. She hasn't paid the bills _____ two months.

15. She hasn't polished the silver _____ last week.

MAKE IT WORK

Fill in the blanks. Tell about yourself.

I haven't _____ for _____.

I haven't _____ since _____.

SHE HASN'T WASHED THE CLOTHES SINCE MONDAY.

Negative Statements with *Since* and *For*

Present Perfect: Regular and Irregular Past Participles

> The last time she washed the clothes was three days ago.
> She hasn't washed the clothes for three days.
>
> The last time they changed the beds was Monday.
> They haven't changed the beds since Monday.
>
> irregular past participles: did → done   fed → fed   paid → paid
> took → taken   wrote → written

PRACTICE

Make negative sentences with *since* or *for*. Begin your sentences with a pronoun.

1. The last time Bill washed the windows was in the summer.
   He hasn't washed the windows since the summer.

2. The last time Bill took out the trash was Thursday.
   _____

3. The last time Roy and Becky cleaned their rooms was two days ago.
   _____

4. The last time Becky fed the dog was yesterday.
   _____

5. The last time Myra washed the clothes was four days ago.
   _____

6. The last time Myra ironed the clothes was Wednesday.
   _____

7. The last time Roy and Becky did the dishes was yesterday.
   _____

8. The last time Roy watered the plants was Thursday.
   _____

9. The last time Bill paid the bills was a month ago.
   _____

10. The last time Myra wrote a letter was two weeks ago.
    _____

HOW MANY TIMES HAS SHE FED THE DOG TODAY?

Questions with *How Many Times*

Present Perfect: Regular and Irregular Past Participles

> Becky feeds the dog.
>
> How many times | **has** she **fed** the dog today?

PRACTICE

Make questions with *how many times*. Use pronouns in your questions.

1. Myra washes the clothes. (this week)

   How many times has she washed the clothes this week?

2. Becky feeds the dog. (today)

   _____

3. Roy and Becky clean their rooms. (this week)

   _____

4. Myra cooks dinner. (this week)

   _____

5. Roy washes the car. (this month)

   _____

6. Roy and Becky clean the bathroom. (this week)

   _____

7. Bill takes out the trash. (this week)

   _____

8. Myra irons the clothes. (this month)

   _____

9. Myra and Becky change the beds. (this month)

   _____

10. Becky dusts the living room. (this week)

    _____

MAKE IT WORK

Answer the questions in complete sentences.

How many times have you washed your hands today?

_____

TIM HAS ALREADY MADE HIS HOTEL RESERVATIONS, BUT JACK HASN'T MADE HIS YET.

Already and ***Yet***

Present Perfect

> Tim has already made his hotel reservations,
> but Jack hasn't made his yet.

Note: Use *already* and *yet* to show that an action was completed at the
moment of speaking.
Use *already* in affirmative statements; use *yet* in negative statements.

PRACTICE

Jack and Tim are going on a trip. Fill in the blanks with *already* or *yet*.

1. Jack has ___already___ picked up his tickets, but Tim hasn't picked his up
   ___yet___.

2. Tim hasn't paid for his tickets _____, but Jack has _____
   paid for his.

3. Jack hasn't gone to the bank _____, and Tim hasn't gone to the
   bank _____ either.

4. Jack has _____ seen his travel agent, but Tim hasn't seen a travel
   agent _____.

5. Both Jack and Tim have _____ gotten their passports.

6. Tim has _____ made his hotel reservations, but Jack hasn't made
   his _____.

7. Jack hasn't gotten insurance _____, but Tim _____ has.

8. Jack has packed his suitcase _____, but Tim hasn't started to pack
   his _____.

9. Both Jack and Tim haven't had time to buy their traveler's checks
   _____.

10. Jack hasn't planned his itinerary _____, but Tim _____ has.

MAKE IT WORK

Complete the sentences with *already* or *yet*. Tell about yourself so far today.

I _____ had lunch _____.

I _____ had dinner _____.

HE HASN'T GONE TO THE BANK YET.

Negative and Affirmative Statements with *Already* and *Yet*

Present Perfect: Regular and Irregular Past Participles

Tim ⬚has⬚ ⬚already⬚ ⬚planned⬚ his itinerary.

He ⬚hasn't seen⬚ a travel agent ⬚yet.⬚

irregular past participles: buy → bought   get → gotten   go → gone
make → made   see → seen

PRACTICE

Look at Tim's list of things to do. Then make sentences with *already* or *yet* and the present perfect. The items that have a check (✔) are things Tim has already done.

> ### *Things to Do*
>
> ✔ plan my itinerary   ✔ make hotel reservations
>   see a travel agent   pay for my plane ticket
> ✔ go to the doctor   pick up my plane ticket
>   go to the bank   ✔ get a passport
>   buy traveler's checks   ✔ take my suit to the cleaners
> ✔ get travel insurance   pack my suitcase

1. *Tim has already planned his itinerary.*
2. *He hasn't seen a travel agent yet.*
3. _____
4. _____
5. _____
6. _____
7. _____
8. _____
9. _____
10. _____
11. _____
12. _____

New Words: itinerary = a plan of a trip, including places to be visited
traveler's checks = special checks sold by a bank to a person who is traveling
insurance = an agreement to pay money in case of an accident

HAS JACK BEEN TO FRANCE YET? YES, HE HAS.

Negative and Affirmative Short Answers

Present Perfect

Has Jack been to France yet?	Yes, he has.
Have Jack and Tim been to France?	Yes, they have.
Has Jack been to Greece?	No, he hasn't.
Have Jack and Tim been to Greece?	No, they haven't.

PRACTICE

Answer the questions with short answers.

Jack and Tim are in Europe now.
They've been there for two weeks.

Jack has already visited England,
France and Germany. Tim has
already visited France and Spain.

1. Are Jack and Tim in Europe now?   _Yes, they are._

2. Have they been there for three weeks?   _No, they haven't._

3. Have they been there for two weeks?   _____

4. Has Jack been to England yet?   _____

5. Has Tim been to England yet?   _____

6. Has Jack visited France yet?   _____

7. Has Tim visited France yet?   _____

8. Have Jack and Tim visited France yet?   _____

9. Has Jack gone to Greece yet?   _____

10. Has Tim gone to Greece yet?   _____

11. Have they been to Greece yet?   _____

12. Has Jack seen Spain yet?   _____

13. Has Tim seen Spain yet?   _____

14. Have Jack and Tim been to Italy yet?   _____

MAKE IT WORK

Answer the question.

Have you been to Europe?   _____

HAVE YOU SEEN IT YET?

Yes-No Questions with *Yet*

Present Perfect: Regular and Irregular Past Participles

I saw the new series on TV last night.

Have you seen it yet?

Has your husband seen it yet?

Have your children seen it yet?

irregular past participles: ate → eaten   met → met   read → read
drove → driven   heard → heard

PRACTICE

Make questions with *yet* and the present perfect.

I saw the new movie at the Strand Theater last night.

1. (you) *Have you seen it yet?* _____

2. (your children) _____

I read K. T. Anders's new book last week.

3. (you) _____

4. (your husband) _____

I met our new neighbors yesterday.

5. (you) _____

6. (your husband) _____

I heard George White's latest compact disc.

7. (your son) _____

8. (you) _____

I drove on the new freeway yesterday.

9. (you) _____

10. (your husband) _____

I saw the new series on TV last night.

11. (your children) _____

12. (you) _____

MAKE IT WORK

Fill in the blank with a question.

I ate at the student cafeteria yesterday. _____ there yet?

HE HASN'T BEEN TO BRAZIL.

Review: Present Perfect

He 's been to Egypt.

He hasn't been to Brazil.

Note: Use the present perfect for an action completed in the past without a
specific time given.

irregular past participle: is/are   was/were → been

P R A C T I C E

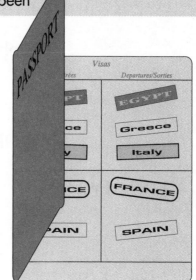

Look at John Burn's passport on
the right. Tell which countries
he's been to and which countries
he hasn't been to.

1. Egypt _He's been to Egypt._ _____

2. England _____

3. the Netherlands _____

4. Greece _____

5. Morocco _____

6. Israel _____

7. France _____

8. Germany _____

9. Spain _____

10. the Republic of China _____

11. Japan _____

12. Italy _____

MAKE IT WORK

Answer the question.

What countries have you been to?

_____

Contrast: Present Perfect, Past, Present

Olga Gomez
5275 High Street
Dallas, Texas

Telephone: (241) 555-8830

RÉSUMÉ

WORK EXPERIENCE

1/89 – Present	Bilingual Secretary A. B. C. Corporation Dallas, Texas
1/85 – 1/89	Secretary Selby Corporation Houston, Texas
1/83 – 1/85	Receptionist United Corporation Santa Fe, New Mexico
1/81 – 1/83	Clerk Typist Sandor, Incorporated Carlsbad, New Mexico

Abbreviations: 1/89 = January 1989

1/20/89 = January 20, 1989

SHE'S BEEN A SECRETARY SINCE 1985.

She	's	a bilingual secretary.
She	was	a secretary from 1985 to 1989.
She	's been	a secretary since 1985.

Note: Use the present perfect for actions that began in the past and continue up to the present. Use the past tense for actions that began in the past and ended in the past.

PRACTICE

Look at the résumé on page 66. Then fill in the blanks with the present perfect, the past, or the present tense. Use contractions whenever possible.

1. (be) She _'s_____ a bilingual secretary at the present time.

2. (be) She _was_____ a secretary from 1985 to 1989.

3. (be) She _'s been_____ a secretary since 1985.

4. (be) She _____ a bilingual secretary since 1989.

5. (work) She _____ in Dallas at the present time.

6. (work) She _____ for A. B. C. Corporation.

7. (start) She _____ her job at A. B. C. Corporation in 1989.

8. (work) She _____ for A. B. C. Corporation since 1989.

9. (work) From 1985 to 1989, she _____ in Houston.

10. (work) She _____ for Selby Corporation.

11. (live) She _____ in Houston for four years.

12. (live) She _____ in Dallas at the present time.

13. (live) She _____ in Dallas since 1989.

14. (live) She _____ in Texas since 1985.

15. (work) From 1983 to 1985, she _____ as a receptionist.

16. (work) She _____ for United Corporation from 1983 to 1985.

17. (live) She _____ in Santa Fe at that time.

18. (be) Before that she _____ a clerk typist.

19. (live) She _____ in Carlsbad in 1982.

20. (work) She _____ for Sandor, Incorporated at that time.

HE'S MARRIED. HE'S BEEN MARRIED SINCE 1984.

Contrast: Present Perfect, Past, Present

```
           PROFILE  OF  HENRY  ORTEGA

Born:                   April 3, 1960

Birthplace:             Mexico City, Mexico

Residence:              Los Angeles, California, 1970 to present

Education:              Hollywood High School, Hollywood, California
                        Diploma, 1978

Profession:             Assistant Television Producer, 1980 to present

Place of Employment:    KTLA Television Station, 1988 to present

Family:                 Wife, Lydia; married 1984 to present
                        Two children: Sally, age 5; Ricardo, age 8

Hobbies:                Collects baseball cards, 1970 to present

Goal:                   To be a TV producer someday
```

HE'S MARRIED. HE'S BEEN MARRIED SINCE 1984.

He	collected	baseball cards in 1970.
He still	collects	baseball cards.
He	's collected	baseball cards since 1970.

PRACTICE

Read the profile on page 68. Then make sentences about Henry Ortega.
Use contractions whenever possible.

Born

1. _He was born on_ _____ April 3, 1960.

Birthplace

2. _____

Residence

3. _____ in Los Angeles.

4 _____ since 1970.

Education

5. _____ Hollywood High School.

6. _____ in 1978.

Profession

7. _____ assistant television producer.

8. _____ since 1980.

Place of Employment

9. _____ for KTLA Television Station.

10. _____ since 1988.

Family

11. _____

12. _____ in 1984.

13. _____ since 1984.

14. _____ two children.

Hobbies

15. _____ baseball cards.

16. _____ in 1970.

17. _____ since 1970.

Goal

18. _____

IN 1952, I WROTE A BOOK ABOUT SPAIN.
I'VE WRITTEN SEVERAL OTHER BOOKS ABOUT TRAVEL.

Contrast: Present Form, Past Form, Past Participle

I write books.
In 1952 I wrote a book about Spain.
I 've written several other books about travel.

irregular forms:	present form	past form	past participle
	am/is/are	was/were	been
	become(s)	became	become
	do/does	did	done
	drive(s)	drove	driven
	get(s)	got	gotten
	go/goes	went	gone
	have/has	had	had
	see(s)	saw	seen
	take(s)	took	taken
	write(s)	wrote	written

PRACTICE

Fill in the blanks with the correct form of the verb. Read the entire story before you begin.

Today is my seventieth birthday. When I look back on the last seventy

years, I think about all the things I've _____*done*_____ in my lifetime. I've
                                    (1. do)

_____ to college, and I've _____ the world. I've
(2. go)   (3. see)

_____ to twenty countries. I've _____ across the
(4. be)   (5. drive)

Sahara Desert, and I've _____ a boat up the Nile River. Of course,
                        (6. take)

I _____ this when I was very young. I _____ to Africa
  (7. do)   (8. go)

in 1946. I've _____ in two foreign countries: Spain and Colombia.
              (9. live)

I _____ a book about my experiences in Spain in 1952. I've also
  (10. write)

_____ several other books about travel.
(11. write)

IN 1952, I WROTE A BOOK ABOUT SPAIN.
I'VE WRITTEN SEVERAL OTHER BOOKS ABOUT TRAVEL.

I've _____ for forty-eight years, and I still _____
    (12. work)   (13. work)

every day. I've _____ nine times, and I've _____
               (14. move)   (15. have)

thirteen different jobs. I _____ English courses in college, so most
                           (16. take)

of my jobs have _____ in writing and publishing.
               (17. be)

I've _____ married twice. My first husband _____
        (18. be)   (19. die)

in 1975. I _____ married again in 1980, and I _____
          (20. get)   (21. be)

still married. I _____ four children and six grandchildren. Last
             (22. have)

month, one of my grandchildren _____ a baby, and I
                           (23. have)

_____ a great-grandmother for the first time.
(24. become)

MAKE IT WORK

Tell four things you've done in your lifetime without mentioning exact times or dates.

I've had six different jobs.

_____

_____

_____

New Word: publishing = business or profession involved in writing and
printing books, magazines, or newspapers
to sell to the public

HE'S BEEN DOING HIS HOMEWORK FOR TWO HOURS.
HE'S DONE FIVE EXERCISES SO FAR.

Contrast: Present Perfect vs. Present Perfect Continuous

He's doing his homework now.

He **'s been doing** his homework for two hours.

He **'s done** five exercises so far.

Note: Use the present perfect continuous for actions not completed at the moment of speaking. Use the present perfect for actions completed at the moment of speaking. Use both the present perfect continuous and the present perfect for actions that began in the past and continue up to the present.

PRACTICE

Make sentences with the present perfect continuous and the present perfect for each situation. Use pronouns and contractions.

Bill is reading a book.

1. _He's been reading_____ a book for two hours.

2. _He's read_____ forty pages so far.

Florie and Bob are traveling in Europe.

3. _____ in Europe for two months.

4. _____ to six countries so far.

Chang is writing letters.

5. _____ six letters so far.

6. _____ letters for two hours.

Jane and Dorothy are driving to work.

7. _____ forty miles so far.

8. _____ for an hour.

Myra is cleaning the house.

9. _____ the house for two hours.

10. _____ the bathroom and the kitchen so far.

Susan is playing tennis.

11. _____ tennis for two hours.

12. _____ six games so far.

WOULD YOU REPEAT THAT? I DON'T UNDERSTAND.

Polite Requests with *Would* and *Could*

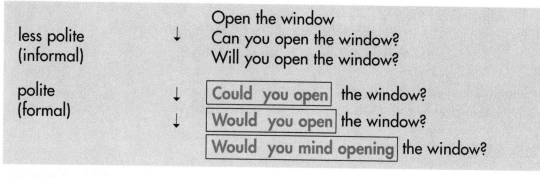

less polite (informal)	↓	Open the window Can you open the window? Will you open the window?
polite (formal)	↓ ↓	Could you open the window? Would you open the window? Would you mind opening the window?

PRACTICE

Read each situation and then make a polite request with *could* or *would*.

1. You are in class. The teacher says something you don't understand. Ask the teacher to repeat it.

   Would you repeat that? I don't understand.

2. The radio next door is loud. Ask your neighbor to turn the radio down.

   _____

3. You need some help with your homework. Ask a classmate to help you with your homework.

   _____

4. You and a co-worker are at a restaurant. Ask her to pass the salt.

   _____

5. You are in your office. As a co-worker is leaving, ask her to shut the door.

   _____

6. You are at a full-service gas station. You want the attendant to fill your car up with gasoline. Ask him to fill it up with regular gas.

   _____

7. You need a ride to the airport. Ask a friend to drive you there.

   _____

MAKE IT WORK

Rewrite these sentences. Make the requests polite.

Are you going to open the door for me?

_____

I want you to sign your name here.

_____

YOU DON'T HAVE TO WORK AT NIGHT.

Have To and *Don't Have To*

> You [have to work] eight hours a day.
> You [don't have to work] at night.

Note: Use *have to* to express necessity.
Use *don't have to* to express lack of necessity.

PRACTICE

Look at the advertisement for a secretary below. Then make sentences with *you have to* and *you don't have to.*

> **Secretary**
> Experience necessary. Type letters, answer the phone, etc. Full time, 8:30 – 5:30, five days a week. No overtime. No computer skills necessary. Good benefits. Paid holidays.
> Send Résumé to Box 25, Star Daily Newspaper, Winston Salem, NC 27106

1. type letters   *You have to type letters.*

2. answer the phone   _____

3. work at night   _____

4. work eight hours a day   _____

5. work overtime   _____

6. work five days a week   _____

7. work on holidays   _____

8. work on Sundays   _____

9. have experience   _____

10. use a computer   _____

MAKE IT WORK

Name three things you have to do at work.

I have to use a computer.

_____

_____

_____

A MECHANIC HAS TO BE ABLE TO FIX CARS.

Be Able To

A mechanic has to $\boxed{\text{be able to fix}}$ cars.

A cashier has to $\boxed{\text{be able to use}}$ a cash register.

Note: Use *be able to* + the simple form of the verb to talk about ability.

PRACTICE

Look at the chart below. Then make sentences with *has to be able to*.

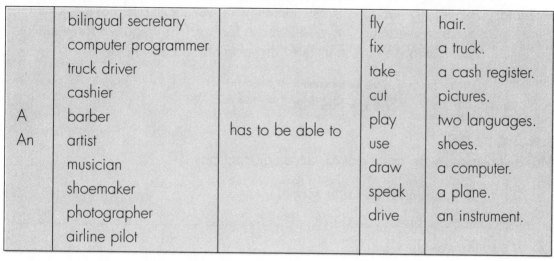

| A An | bilingual secretary
computer programmer
truck driver
cashier
barber
artist
musician
shoemaker
photographer
airline pilot | has to be able to | fly
fix
take
cut
play
use
draw
speak
drive | hair.
a truck.
a cash register.
pictures.
two languages.
shoes.
a computer.
a plane.
an instrument. |

1. *A bilingual secretary has to be able to speak two languages.*

2. _____

3. _____

4. _____

5. _____

6. _____

7. _____

8. _____

9. _____

10. _____

I'VE GOT TO GO TO CLASS.

Have Got To

I	've		
You	've		
He	's		
She	's	got to go	to class.
We	've		
They	've		

Note: Use *have got to* to express necessity. *Have got to* and *have to* are similar in meaning; *have to* is more formal. The negative form of *have got to* isn't used. Instead use *don't* or *doesn't have to*.

contractions: I've = I have
            She's = She has

PRACTICE
Make sentences with *have got to*. Use contractions.

1. It's 3:00. (pick up the kids at school)
   She *'s got to pick up the kids at school.*_____

2. It's 10:00. (go to class)
   They _____

3. It's 4:50. (mail a letter before 5:00)
   He _____

4. It's 2:30. (go to the bank before 3:00)
   I _____

5. It's 2:30. (get to the wedding on time)
   We _____

6. It's 5:30. (catch the train)
   She _____

7. It's 5:30. (pick up his wife)
   He _____

8. It's 4:30. (leave work early)
   I _____

9. It's 6:30. (be home before dark)
   They _____

10. It's 11:00. (go to bed)
    You _____

YOU MUST NOT THROW TRASH ON THE HIGHWAY.

Must and Must Not

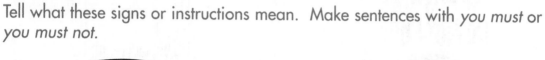

 You must obey the sign.
You must not enter this property.

Note: Use *must* to express necessity or obligation.
Use *must not* to express prohibition. Do not
use *to* after *must*.

contraction: mustn't = must not

PRACTICE

Tell what these signs or instructions mean. Make sentences with *you must* or
you must not.

1. <u>You must not eat</u>
   or drink this.

2. _____
   here.

3. _____
   your seatbelt.

4. _____
   your radio here.

5. _____ or put
   25¢ in the slot.

6. _____

7. _____
a gun on the plane.

8. _____
the bill on or before January 15th.

9. _____
this area.

10. _____
a permit to fish here.

$500 Fine
for
Littering
Highway

11. _____
or leave by this door.

12. _____
or throw trash on the highway. If
you do, you might have to pay $500.

MAKE IT WORK

Name something you must not do in a theater.

_____

Name something you must have to leave a country.

_____

Name something you must have if you want to drive.

_____

YOU DON'T HAVE TO STOP, BUT YOU MUST NOT SPEED.

Contrast: *Don't Have To vs. Must Not*

You | must not drive | faster than 55 miles an hour.
You | don't have to drive | 55 miles an hour. You can drive slower.

Note: must not = prohibited   don't have to = not necessary

PRACTICE

Look at the signs. Then fill in the blanks with *don't have to* or *must not*.

1. You <u>*must not*</u> drive faster than 25 miles an hour.

2. You _____ drive 25 miles an hour. You can drive slower.

3. You must slow down, but you _____ stop.

4. You _____ speed.

5. If a train is coming, you _____ go.

6. If there's no train coming, you _____ stop, but you should slow down.

7. You _____ speed.

8. You must slow down, but you _____ stop.

9. You _____ stop.

10. You must slow down. You _____ drive faster than 25 miles an hour.

Equivalent: mile = 1.6 kilometers

YOU AREN'T ALLOWED TO PLAY YOUR RADIO HERE.

Be Allowed To

You aren't allowed to play your radio here.

Note: aren't allowed to = not permitted to

PRACTICE

Make sentences with *you aren't allowed to.*

1. No roller skating here.

   You aren't allowed to roller skate here.

2. This is a non-smoking restaurant.

   _____

3. No fishing on the lake.

   _____

4. No ice-skating on the lake.

   _____

5. No littering the highway.

   _____

6. No radio playing on the bus.

   _____

7. No bicycle riding in the park.

   _____

8. No hunting here.

   _____

9. No trespassing on this property.

   _____

10. No camping on the beach.

    _____

11. No parking here.

    _____

12. No swimming here.

    _____

New Word: trespass = wrongly enter land or property of another person

SHE'D BETTER NOT WALK HOME ALONE.

Had Better and *Had Better Not*

Mary had better study for her exam (or she'll fail).
She 'd better not go to the party tonight.

Note: Use *had better* to express strong advice. It expresses the idea that something bad will happen if you don't follow the advice.

contractions: she'd better = she had better

she'd better not = she had better not

PRACTICE

Read each situation. Then give advice, first with *had better not* and then with *had better*. Use contractions.

It's very late at night. A group of Mary's friends offer to walk home with her, but she wants to walk home alone.

1. *She'd better not walk home alone.*
2. *She'd better walk with her friends.*

A friend has bought some shoes in a department store. He takes out his wallet to pay for the shoes and leaves his wallet on the counter.

3. _____
4. _____

A friend is leaving her house. As she walks away, she leaves the door unlocked.

5. _____
6. _____

A friend is going to walk home late at night. She refuses to take a taxi.

7. _____
8. _____

A friend parks his car on the street. He leaves his camera in the car.

9. _____
10. _____

A friend is going away on a vacation. She locks the door of her apartment, but she leaves the windows open.

11. _____
12. _____

YOU SHOULD BE ON TIME.

Should and Shouldn't

When you have a business appointment, you should be on time.

When you have a job interview, you shouldn't be late.

Note: Use *should* for advice or suggestions.

weakest

↓ You should be on time.
↓ You had better be on time.
↓ You have to be on time.

strongest   Be on time.

Do not use *to* after *should*.   contraction: shouldn't = should not

PRACTICE

Read each situation. Then give advice with *you should* or *you shouldn't*.

When you are invited to a wedding,

1. *You should answer* _____ the invitation.

2. _____ late.

3. _____ fancy clothes.

4. _____ a gift.

When you are invited to dinner,

5. _____ late.

6. _____ a gift, like wine or flowers.

When you are at the dinner table,

7. _____ until the hostess starts to eat.

8. _____ with your mouth open.

When you receive a gift,

9. _____ "I don't like it."

10. _____ "Thank you."

When you are invited to spend the weekend at someone's house,

11. _____ a gift.

12. _____ a thank-you note afterward.

IT MIGHT RAIN TOMORROW.

Might and *Will*

There's a 40% chance of rain tomorrow.
It | might rain | tomorrow.

There's a 70% chance of rain tomorrow.
It | will probably rain | tomorrow.

There's a 100% chance of rain tomorrow.
It | will rain | tomorrow.

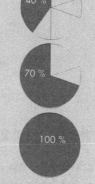

Note: Use *might* to express possibility when you are not certain of something. The negative of *might* = *might not*. Do not contract *might not*.

PRACTICE

Make sentences with *might, will probably,* and *will.*

1. There's a 60% chance of fog tomorrow.
   It will probably be foggy tomorrow.

2. There's a 30% chance of rain tomorrow.
   _____

3. There's a 50% chance of warm air moving in tomorrow.
   _____

4. There's a 100% chance of nice weather tomorrow.
   _____

5. There's a 40% chance of clouds tomorrow.
   _____

6. There's a 70% chance of wind tomorrow.
   _____

7. There's a 40% chance of fog tomorrow.
   _____

8. There's a 30% chance of snow tomorrow.
   _____

9. There's an 80% chance of cold air moving in tomorrow.
   _____

10. There's a 100% chance of sun tomorrow.
    _____

SHE MUST BE AN ACCOUNTANT.

Assumptions with *Must*

What is he?	He might be an accountant.	You are 50% sure.
	He **must be** an accountant.	You are 95% sure.
	He is an accountant.	You are 100% sure.

Note: Use *must* to express an assumption when you are almost sure that it's true.

PRACTICE

Make guesses or assumptions about each person's occupation. Choose from the list below.

police officer	painter	dancer	✔ cowboy
carpenter	boxer	doctor	musician
business executive	waitress		

1. He's wearing jeans, a big hat, and boots.

   He must be a cowboy.

2. He's wearing a white uniform, and he's carrying a black bag.

   _____

3. She's wearing a dark uniform, and she's carrying a gun.

   _____

4. He has paint all over his jeans.

   _____

5. He has a broken jaw, and his eye is black and blue.

   _____

6. She's wearing a black uniform with a white apron.

   _____

7. She has a suit on, and she's carrying a briefcase.

   _____

8. He's wearing a black suit and a bow tie. He's carrying a violin.

   _____

9. He's wearing ballet shoes and a black leotard.

   _____

10. He has overalls on, and he's carrying a hammer.

   _____

SHE'D RATHER EAT AT A RESTAURANT.

Would Rather and *Would Rather Not*

Would Karen rather eat at home or at a restaurant?

She ⌈'d rather eat⌉ at a restaurant.

She ⌈'d rather not cook.⌉

Note: Use *would rather* to express a preference where a choice is given.
contractions: she'd = she would   I'd = I would

PRACTICE

Look at the dialogue below. Then fill in the blanks with *would rather* or *would rather not*. Use contractions with pronouns.

Karen: Would you rather eat at home or at a restaurant?
Charlie: I'd rather eat at home.
Karen: I'd rather not cook dinner. Let's eat out. Afterwards, let's go
              to a movie.
Charlie: I'd rather not. Let's watch television.
Karen: Let's compromise. We'll eat out, and then we'll go home.
              Would you rather eat Chinese food or Italian food?
Charlie: I'd rather eat Italian food.

1. Charlie _would rather not eat_____ at a restaurant.

2. He _____ at home.

3. Karen _____ at home.

4. She _____ at a restaurant.

5. She _____ dinner.

6. Charlie _____ Italian food.

7. Karen _____ television at home.

8. She _____ to a movie.

9. Charlie _____ to a movie.

10. He _____ television.

MAKE IT WORK

Tell which of the following things you'd rather do.

eat Chinese food or Italian food

_____

go to a movie or rent a video and watch it on television

_____

I'D RATHER GO TO A FANCY RESTAURANT.

Contrast: *Would Like* vs. *Would Rather*

Would you like to go to Wong's Restaurant?	No, I wouldn't.
Would you like to go to Ming's Restaurant?	Yes, I would.
Would you like to go to Ming's or Wong's?	I'd rather go to Ming's.

Note: *Would like* expresses preference when there is usually one choice.
Would rather expresses preference when there is more than one choice.

PRACTICE

Answer the questions. Tell about yourself.

1. Would you like to eat out tonight?
   <u>Yes, I would.   OR   No, I wouldn't.</u>

2. Would you like to have pizza?
   _____

3. Would you rather eat French food or Italian food?
   _____

4. Would you rather have pizza or steak?
   _____

5. Would you like to get dressed up tonight?
   _____

6. Would you rather go to a fancy restaurant or a casual restaurant?
   _____

7. Would you like to do something afterwards?
   _____

8. Would you rather go somewhere or stay at home?
   _____

9. Would you like to watch television?
   _____

10. Would you rather go to a movie or watch television?
    _____

MAKE IT WORK

Ask a friend to eat out tonight. Then ask which restaurant he would prefer.

■ _____ ?

☐ Yes, I would.

■ _____ ?

☐ I'd rather go to a French restaurant.

86

SHE SHOULD TAKE A RAINCOAT. IT MIGHT RAIN.

Review: Modals and Idiomatic Modals

| She | shouldn't take | a bathrobe. | It | won't fit | in her suitcase. |
| She | should take | a raincoat. | It | might rain. | |

PRACTICE

Read the information below about the tour of San Francisco. Marilyn is going on the tour. Tell which of the items below Marilyn should take and which she shouldn't take with her. Then give a reason.

Four Day Bus Tour to San Francisco

Hotel: The elegant Grand Hotel on San Francisco Bay
Weather: 51– 66°F; windy with a 50% chance of rain
Luggage: Only one small suitcase per person is allowed.

---

1. a lot of cash   _She shouldn't take a lot of cash._
                           Someone might steal it.

2. an umbrella

3. a lot of extra clothes

4. a sweater

5. a fancy dress

6. her valuable jewelry

7. a bathing suit

8. some walking shoes

9. a fur coat

10. a scarf

YOU'D BETTER NOT TAKE A LOT OF CASH.

Review: Modals and Idiomatic Modals

advice		certainty	
weakest ↓ ↓ ↓ **strongest**	should had better have to/have got to, must	**weakest** ↓ ↓ ↓ **strongest**	might must will

Mary is going on a tour to Paris, France.

advice

She should take a camera.

She shouldn't take a lot of extra clothes.

She 'd better take some traveler's checks.

She 'd better not take a lot of cash.

obligation/necessity

She 's got to get a new passport.

She has to take a passport.

She must take a passport.

prohibition

She must not travel without one.

She isn't allowed to travel without one.

not necessary

She doesn't have to have a passport if she travels in the United States.

possibility

The weather might be cold in Paris.

It might not be very warm.

assumption

She must like to travel with other people, since she's going on a tour.

She must not like to travel alone.

PRACTICE

Read each situation. Then make an appropriate response. First write an affirmative sentence, then a negative one. Use contractions whenever possible.

Your friend is sick, but he plans to go to work tomorrow. Give him advice.

1. You _'d better stay_ _____ home tomorrow.

2. You _'d better not go_ _____ to work.

YOU'D BETTER NOT TAKE A LOT OF CASH.

Your friend wants to open a checking account at the bank. Tell him what he needs to do.

3. You _____ some money in the account.

4. You _____ a lot of money in the account.
   Ten dollars is enough.

A friend bought a new radio, but it doesn't work. Give her some advice.

5. You _____ it back to the store.

6. You _____ it.

You and a friend are at the library. Your friend starts to smoke a cigarette. Smoking is prohibited in the library. Tell your friend to smoke outside.

7. If you want to smoke, you _____ outside.

8. You _____ in the library.

Your friend is failing his English course. He wants to go to a party tonight. Give him some advice.

9. You _____ your English, or you'll fail the exam.

10. You _____ to the party.

You have a two-week vacation at work. You're thinking of going to Paris, but you're not sure if you'll go anywhere. A friend asks you what your plans are for your vacation. Tell him your possible plans.

11. I _____ to Paris.

12. I _____ anywhere. I haven't decided.

Your friend got up at 4:00 A. M. He worked hard all day. Make two assumptions about your friend.

13. He _____ tired.

14. (feel) He _____ like going out tonight.

MAKE IT WORK

Complete the sentences about yourself.

I should _____

I'd better _____

I have to _____

I might _____

THEY HAD TO CLEAN THE ENTIRE HOUSE.

Had To

> The inside of the house needed paint.
>
> They had to paint the inside of the house.
>
> Note: Use *had to* for past obligation.
> *Had to* is used as the past of *must* for obligation.

PRACTICE

When Paula and Laura bought a house a year ago, it needed a lot of work. Below are some of the things they had to do before they moved into the house. Make sentences with *had to*.

1. The entire house was a mess. (clean)

   They had to clean the entire house.

2. All the windows were dirty. (wash)

   _____

3. The house had no window screens. (put in)

   _____

4. The stove was in bad condition. (fix)

   _____

5. There wasn't a refrigerator. (buy)

   _____

6. The kitchen didn't have a counter. (build)

   _____

7. The inside of the house needed to be painted. (paint)

   _____

8. There were no light fixtures. (put in)

   _____

MAKE IT WORK

When you moved into your apartment or house, what things did you have to do?

_____

_____

New Words: window screen   light fixture

HE DIDN'T HAVE TO BUY A NEW STOVE.

Didn't Have To

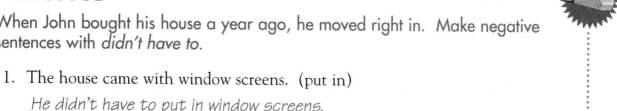

The house came with a new stove.

He didn't have to buy a new stove when he moved in.

Note: Use *didn't have to* for lack of necessity in the past.

PRACTICE

When John bought his house a year ago, he moved right in. Make negative sentences with *didn't have to.*

1. The house came with window screens. (put in)

   He didn't have to put in window screens.

2. It came with a refrigerator. (buy)

   _____

3. It came with a new stove. (buy)

   _____

4. It had a large counter in the kitchen. (build)

   _____

5. The inside of the house didn't need paint. (paint)

   _____

6. The roof wasn't in bad condition. (fix)

   _____

7. It came with new light fixtures. (put in)

   _____

8. It had new rugs. (buy)

   _____

9. It had an air conditioner. (put in)

   _____

10. The windows were clean. (wash)

    _____

MAKE IT WORK

Name two things you didn't have to do when you moved into your house or apartment.

_____

_____

HE COULD READ WITHOUT HIS GLASSES TEN YEARS AGO.

Past Ability with *Could*

He can't read without his glasses.

He could read without his glasses ten years ago.

Note: Use *could* to express ability in the past tense.

PRACTICE

Make sentences with *could*.

1. My father can't swim a mile.

   He could swim a mile _____ ten years ago.

2. My father can't play tennis all day.

   _____ ten years ago.

3. My father can't read without his glasses.

   _____ ten years ago.

4. My father can't go out every night.

   _____ ten years ago.

5. My father can't stay up all night.

   _____ ten years ago.

6. My father can't run up and down the stairs.

   _____ ten years ago.

7. My father can't lift heavy boxes.

   _____ ten years ago.

8. My father can't eat rich food.

   _____ ten years ago.

9. My father can't work for twelve hours a day.

   _____ ten years ago.

10. My father can't run a mile in fifteen minutes.

    _____ ten years ago.

MAKE IT WORK

What could you do ten years ago that you can't do now?

I could stay up all night. _____

_____

_____

SHE SHOULD HAVE TAKEN HER MONEY WITH HER.

Should Have

> She didn't turn down the heat before she left the house.
>
> She should have turned down the heat before she left the house.
>
> Note: Use *should* + *have* + the past participle to express an action that was advisable but did not occur.
>
> irregular past participles: feed → fed   make → made   take → taken

PRACTICE

Angela left the house in a hurry. Make sentences with *should have*.

1. She didn't turn down the heat.

    She should have turned down the heat.

2. She didn't turn off the lights.

    _____

3. She didn't feed the dog.

    _____

4. She didn't close the windows.

    _____

5. She didn't take out the trash.

    _____

6. She didn't make sure the oven was off.

    _____

7. She didn't turn off the radio.

    _____

8. She didn't lock all the doors.

    _____

9. She didn't take her keys with her.

    _____

10. She didn't take her money with her.

    _____

MAKE IT WORK

Name two things you should have done before you left the house today.

_____

_____

WE COULDN'T GO ANYWHERE.

Review: *Couldn't* vs. *Had To*

> There wasn't any public transportation.
>
> We | couldn't go | anywhere.
>
> We | had to stay | at home.
>
> Note: Use *couldn't* + the simple form of the verb; use *had* + the infinitive.
>
> could = ability   had to = necessity
>
> contraction: couldn't = could not

PRACTICE

Fill in the blanks with *couldn't* or *had to*. Be sure to read the entire sentence first.

There was a terrible snowstorm in New Jersey last winter. The town my

family and I live in had nine feet of snow. It was so cold that we

_____couldn't start_____ our car. There wasn't any public transportation, so we
    (1. start)

_____ anywhere by bus. When we wanted to go somewhere,
    (2. go)

we _____ . A few grocery stores were open, but there weren't
    (3. walk)

any food deliveries. We _____ any fresh food, such as milk,
                              (4. buy)

bread, or vegetables. We _____ canned food. The telephones
                              (5. buy)

were out of order, so we _____ our telephone. We
                              (6. use)

_____ cold showers because there wasn't any hot water. There
    (7. take)

wasn't any electricity either. We _____ the lights. We
                                        (8. use)

_____ candles at night. Of course, we _____
    (9. use)   (10. watch)

television. Because the stove is electric, it wasn't working either. We

_____ anything. We _____ cold food for two days.
    (11. cook)   (12. eat)

New Words: canned food = food in cans   candle

out of order = not working

94

APPLES ARE GROWN IN WASHINGTON.

Affirmative Statements
Passive Present

> Apples | are grown | in Washington.
> Washington | is known | for its apples.

Note: Use *am, is,* or *are* + the past participle to form the passive voice.

Regular participles are formed by adding *d* or *ed* to the simple form of the verb.

irregular past participles: eat → eaten   grow → grown
                             know → known   make → made

PRACTICE

Fill in the blanks with the passive present.

1. (grow) Apples _____*are grown*_____ in New York and California.

2. (know) However, the state of Washington _____ for its apples.

3. (grow) Usually apples _____ in fields or orchards.

4. (cover) In the spring, the apple trees _____ with white flowers.

5. (pick) The apples _____ in the fall.

6. (pack) Then they _____ into large wooden boxes.

7. (deliver) The best apples _____ to stores.

8. (sell) They _____ at supermarkets.

9. (consume) Millions of apples _____ each year.

10. (use) Some _____ for making apple juice.

11. (eat) Others _____ raw.

12. (use) Many _____ for baking.

MAKE IT WORK

Name two things that are made or grown in your country.

_____

_____

New Word: consume = eat or use

THE INJURED PEOPLE WERE TAKEN TO THE HOSPITAL.

Affirmative Statements

Passive Past

> The injured person | was taken | to the hospital.
>
> The injured people | were taken | to the hospital.
>
> Note: Use *was* or *were* + the past participle to form the
> passive past.
>
> irregular past participles: hit → hit   put → put
>   hurt → hurt   take → taken

PRACTICE

Fill in the blanks with the passive past.

DAILY NEWSPAPER

SIX PEOPLE KILLED IN AUTO ACCIDENT

Tuesday, Dec. 19—Six people ___*were killed*___
                                    (1. kill)

in an accident on the Santa Monica Freeway

yesterday. Seventeen other people _____. Six trucks and
                                           (2. hurt)

seventeen cars _____.
                    (3. involve)

The accident occurred shortly after 8:00 P.M. when a truck

_____ by another truck. Then the two trucks
      (4. hit)

_____ by several other cars. The cars and trucks caught fire.
      (5. hit)

Some of the people _____ by other cars when they tried to
                          (6. injure)

escape the fire. An ambulance _____ to the scene and fire
                                      (7. call)

trucks _____. Then the state police _____.
            (8. notify)   (9. notify)

The fire _____ at about noon yesterday. The injured people
              (10. put out)

_____ to the hospital. The freeway _____
      (11. take)   (12. close)

to traffic all day.

New Words: catch fire = start to burn
                escape = get away; reach freedom
                freeway = highway

HER JEWELRY WAS TAKEN.

Review: Passive Past

Someone took her jewelry.   Her jewelry was taken.

Note: Use the passive when you don't know who did the action.

irregular past participles: broke → broken   left → left
                              found → found   stole → stolen
                              threw → thrown

PRACTICE

Read about the robbery. Then rewrite the sentences. Use the passive past.

Last Saturday evening, someone robbed Ellen Downing. Shortly after midnight, someone broke into her house. Someone broke the downstairs windows. Someone threw her clothes everywhere. Someone unlocked her jewelry box. Someone took her gold jewelry. Someone stole her compact disc player and her television. Someone took some money. Someone left the front door open. Someone in the neighborhood called the police.

Last Saturday evening, Ellen Downing was robbed.

_____

_____

_____

_____

_____

_____

_____

_____

_____

_____

_____

_____

_____

New Word: break into = enter a building by force

THE MOVIE WAS BORING.

Adjectives Ending in *-ed* and *-ing*

Past of the Verb *To Be*

> The movie bored Dave.
>
> Dave was bored. The movie was boring.

PRACTICE

Dave and Phil went to the new movie, "The Sharks." Complete the sentences with the correct form of the adjective.

The movie didn't interest Dave.

1. Dave *wasn't interested.*
2. The movie _____

The sharks frightened Dave.

3. The sharks _____
4. Dave _____

The plot confused Dave.

5. The plot _____
6. Dave _____

The violence shocked Dave.

7. Dave _____
8. The violence _____

On the other hand, the movie entertained Phil.

9. Phil _____
10. The movie _____

The plot fascinated Phil.

11. The plot _____
12. Phil _____

The ending surprised Phil.

13. Phil _____
14. The ending _____

MAKE IT WORK

Fill in the dialogue. Use adjectives from the Practice above.

Phil: Wasn't *The Sharks* an _____ movie?

Dave: I didn't think so. I thought the movie was _____.

Phil: Weren't you _____ by the ending?

Dave: No. I was _____.

New Words: plot = plan of a story   violence = rough physical force

I WAS DISAPPOINTED.

Adjectives Ending in *-ed* and *-ing*

Verb *To Be*

I thought it was	boring.	I was	bored.
It was	disappointing.	I was	disappointed.

PRACTICE

Fill in the dialogue with the correct adjective form of the word in parentheses.

Dave: Wasn't Wonder World Amusement Park _____*boring*_____?
(1. bore)

Phil: Were you _____? I thought it was great. The roller
(2. bore)

coaster ride was really _____.
(3. excite)

Dave: I didn't think so. I was _____.
(4. disappoint)

Phil: Did you like the train ride around the park?

Dave: No. I thought it was _____.
(5. bore)

Phil: You liked the boat ride, didn't you?

Dave: No. We had to wait in line for an hour.

By the time I got on the boat, I was _____.
(6. exhaust)

Phil: What about the Wild Water Show? It was _____!
(7. amaze)

Dave: I wasn't _____. I thought it was _____.
(8. amaze) (9. terrify)
You know, the man was almost killed.

Phil: Well, I thought it was very _____.
(10. entertain)

Dave: I thought the most entertaining part of the amusement park was the

restaurant!

MAKE IT WORK

Tell how you feel about the following things. Use adjectives ending in *ed* or *ing*.

horror movies _____

amusement parks _____

THERE ARE A FEW HOTELS IN LAMBERTVILLE.

Quantifiers: *A Little, A Few, A Lot Of*

There is and *There Are*

Facts about the City of Lambertville

air pollution	2%
antique shops	25
apartment buildings	53
churches	3
crime	3 criminal offenses per year
grocery stores	2
hotels	3
industry	1%
museums	2
office buildings	2
old houses	150
restaurants	19

New Words: industry = large business
air pollution = air that is not clean or pure

THERE ARE A FEW HOTELS IN LAMBERTVILLE.

There are a lot of restaurants in Lambertville.

There are a few hotels in Lambertville.

There's a little air pollution in Lambertville.

Note: *a lot of* = a large number   *a little* and *a few* = a small number

Use *a lot of* with both countable and uncountable nouns.

Use *a few* with countable nouns.

Use *a little* with uncountable nouns.   industry   air pollution   crime

PRACTICE

Look at the information on page 100. Then make sentences about Lambertville with *there is* and *there are*. Use *a lot of*, *a few*, or *a little*.

1. *There's a little air pollution in Lambertville.*

2. _____

3. _____

4. _____

5. _____

6. _____

7. _____

8. _____

9. _____

10. _____

11. _____

12. _____

MAKE IT WORK

Tell about your city or town.

_____

_____

_____

_____

THERE ISN'T MUCH NOISE AT NIGHT.

Quantifiers: *Much, Many, Any*

There Is and *There Are*

There aren't | any | movie theaters in Titusville.

There aren't | many | buildings in Titusville.

There isn't | much | noise at night in Titusville.

Note: *any* = none   *aren't many* and *isn't much* = a small number
Use *many* with countable nouns. Use *much* with uncountable nouns.
noise   litter

PRACTICE

Look at the picture below. Then make sentences about Titusville using
there isn't and *there aren't*. Use *much, many,* or *any.*

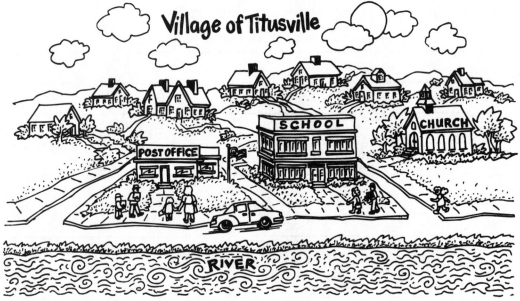

1. people *There aren't many people in Titusville.*

2. shops _____

3. traffic _____

4. hotels _____

5. industry _____

6. buildings _____

7. litter _____

8. apartments _____

9. houses _____

10. hospitals _____

THERE ARE NO DISCOS IN TITUSVILLE.

Quantifiers: *One, No, Any*

There Is and *There Are*

> There's [one] church in Titusville.
> There are [no] discos in Titusville.
> There aren't [any] discos in Titusville.
>
> Note: When you put *no* before a noun, it expresses a negative idea:
> *no* discos.
> Use *any* with a negative verb. There *aren't any* discos.

P R A C T I C E

Look at the picture of Titusville on page 102. Then fill in the blanks with *one*, *no*, or *any*.

1. There aren't _____*any*_____ movie theaters in Titusville.

2. There's _____ school in Titusville.

3. There's _____ litter on the streets in Titusville.

4. There are _____ grocery stores in Titusville.

5. There's _____ church in Titusville.

6. There isn't _____ air pollution in Titusville.

7. There aren't _____ restaurants in Titusville.

8. There are _____ hospitals in Titusville.

9. There aren't _____ department stores in Titusville.

10. There's _____ post office in Titusville.

11. There are _____ highways or freeways in Titusville.

12. There aren't _____ hotels in Titusville.

13. There's _____ industry in Titusville.

14. There aren't _____ office buildings in Titusville.

MAKE IT WORK

Tell about your city or town.

There's one _____

There aren't any _____

There are no _____

THE CLOSET ISN'T LARGE ENOUGH.

Too and *Enough*

Verb *To Be*

> The closet is small.
>
> The closet is | too | small.
>
> The closet isn't large | enough. |
>
> Note: Place *too* before the word it modifies.
>   Place *enough* after the word it modifies.

P R A C T I C E

Add *too* or *enough* to the sentences.

1. My apartment is expensive. (too)

   My apartment is too expensive.

2. My apartment is also small. (too)

   _____

3. The kitchen isn't modern. (enough)

   _____

4. The kitchen is small. (too)

   _____

5. The closets aren't big. (enough)

   _____

6. It isn't close to a shopping area. (enough)

   _____

7. It's far from the bus station. (too)

   _____

8. My street isn't safe. (enough)

   _____

9. The neighborhood is dangerous. (too)

   _____

10. The neighborhood is noisy. (too)

    _____

MAKE IT WORK

Tell one thing wrong with your apartment or house.

_____

SHE'S TOO SHORT TO BE ON THE BASKETBALL TEAM.

Too and *Enough* with Infinitives

Verb *To Be*

> She's `too` short `to be` on the baseketball team.
>
> She isn't tall `enough` `to be` on the baseketball team.

PRACTICE

Make sentences with *too, enough,* and an infinitive.

She can't be on the basketball team.

1. short   *She's too short to be on the basketball team.*

2. tall   *She isn't tall enough to be on the basketball team.*

She can't run on the track team.

3. fast   _____

4. slow   _____

He can't play professional baseball.

5. young   _____

6. old   _____

He can't play on the football team.

7. small   _____

8. big   _____

9. heavy   _____

She can't play on the tennis team.

10. good   _____

11. accurate   _____

12. fast   _____

He can't be on the boxing team.

13. small   _____

14. quick   _____

15. strong   _____

New Words: team = a group of people who do something together, such as play a sport

     track (team) = racing or running (team)

     professional = at a level to make money from an activity, such as a sport

boxer

I THINK YOU WORK VERY HARD.

Adverbs of Manner

Simple Present

I'm not a very graceful dancer.

I think you dance very graceful |ly|.

Note: Add *ly* to form most adverbs of manner.

irregular forms: fast → fast   hard → hard   good → well

PRACTICE

Make sentences with adverbs.

1. I'm not a very good piano player.
   I think you play the piano very well.

2. I'm not a very quick learner.

   _____

3. I'm not a very cautious driver.

   _____

4. I'm not a very fast reader.

   _____

5. I'm not a very neat dresser.

   _____

6. I'm not a very graceful dancer.

   _____

7. I'm not a very good tennis player.

   _____

8. I'm not a very attentive listener.

   _____

9. I'm not a very hard worker.

   _____

10. I'm not a very good swimmer.

    _____

MAKE IT WORK

Fill in the dialogue with a compliment.

■ I can't sing. I don't have a very good voice.

☐ _____

I SPEAK ENGLISH TOO SLOWLY.

Review: Word Order of Adverbs and Adjectives

Present, Present Continuous

	verb	object	adverb of degree	adverb of manner	adverb of degree
I don't	speak	English		fast	enough.
I	speak	English	too	slowly.	

Note: Do not use adverbs of manner between the verb and its object:
Incorrect: I speak slowly English.

PRACTICE

Put the words in the correct order.

1. ■ English/ your / like / class / how / you / do / ?
   How do you like your English class?

2. ☐ it / much / I / very / like / .
   _____

3. very / it's / interesting / .
   _____

4. ■ a / students / of / your / there /lot / are / class / in / ?
   _____

5. ☐ no, / many / students / aren't / there /.
   _____

6. small / it's / class / a / .
   _____

7. ■ learning / you / much / are / English/ ?
   _____

8. ☐ yes, / but / enough / I / fast / speak / don't / .
   _____

9. ■ well / you / I / speak / very / English / think/ .
   _____

MAKE IT WORK

Answer the questions.

How well do you speak English? _____

How well do you understand English? _____

107

YOU SHOULD DRINK LESS ALCOHOL.

Noun Comparisons with *More, Less, Fewer*

Should

You should take | more | vitamins.   You should drink | less | alcohol.

You should eat | more | vegetables.   You should eat | fewer | cookies.

Note: Use *more* with countable and uncountable nouns.
Use *fewer* with countable nouns
Use *less* with uncountable nouns.
alcohol   candy   cheese   coffee   meat   sugar   yogurt   food

PRACTICE

Give someone advice on how to stay healthy. Make sentences with *more, less,* and *fewer.* Begin your sentences with *you.*

1. vitamins   *You should take more vitamins.*

2. candy   *You should eat less candy.*

3. yogurt   _____

4. sugar   _____

5. carrots   _____

6. alcohol   _____

7. potato chips   _____

8. meat   _____

9. milk   _____

10. coffee   _____

11. apples   _____

12. soft drinks   _____

13. cheese   _____

14. cookies   _____

15. low-fat food   _____

MAKE IT WORK

Give someone advice on other ways to stay healthy.

You should get more rest.

_____

_____

THE GRAY CAT ISN'T AS FRIENDLY AS THE BLACK CAT.

As + Adjective + As

Verb *To Be*

> The gray cat is | as old as | the black cat.
>
> The gray cat isn't | as friendly as | the black cat.
>
> Note: Use *as . . . as* with one-, two-, or three-syllable adjectives.
> The verb can be either negative or affirmative.

The Gray Cat	
one year old	graceful
14 inches tall	friendly
9 pounds	playful
17 inches long	clean
gentle	healthy
nice	active
beautiful	

The Black Cat	
one year old	graceful
16 inches tall	very friendly
12 pounds	very playful
19 inches long	clean
gentle	very healthy
nice	active
very beautiful	

PRACTICE

Make sentences about the gray cat. Use *as . . . as*.

1. old   *The gray cat is as old as the black cat.*

2. tall   *The gray cat isn't as tall as the black cat.*

3. heavy   _____

4. long   _____

5. big   _____

6. gentle   _____

7. nice   _____

8. beautiful _____

9. graceful _____

10. friendly _____

11. playful _____

12. clean   _____

13. healthy _____

14. active   _____

MY TIE IS DIFFERENT FROM YOURS.

The Same As and *Different From*
Verb *To Be*

My tie has red stripes.	My tie has red stripes.
Your tie has red stripes.	Your tie has blue stripes
My tie is the same as yours.	My tie is different from yours.

PRACTICE

Make sentences with *the same as* or *different from*.

1. My sweater is wool. Your sweater is nylon.
   My sweater is different from yours.

2. My gloves are brown leather. Your gloves are brown leather.

   _____

3. My umbrella is red. Your umbrella is black.

   _____

4. My ring is gold. Your ring is silver.

   _____

5. My watch is a Timex. Your watch is a Timex.

   _____

6. My slacks are gray wool. Your slacks are gray wool.

   _____

7. My scarf is cotton. Your scarf is silk.

   _____

8. My coat is navy blue wool. Your coat is navy blue wool.

   _____

9. My shirt is silk. Your shirt is polyester.

   _____

10. My wallet is brown leather. Your wallet is black leather.

    _____

MAKE IT WORK

Look at the picture.
Then compare what the
man and the woman
are wearing.

_____

_____

_____

THE APARTMENT IN QUEENS IS CHEAPER.

Adjective Comparatives with *-er* and *More*

Verb *To Be*, Simple Present

The apartment in Queens is	cheaper.	
-er	**-ier**	**more**
cheap → cheap er	sunny → sunn ier	expensive → more expensive
large → large r	pretty → prett ier	
Notes: Add *r* or *er* to most one-syllable adjectives.	Add *er* to most two-syllable adjectives ending in *y*. Change the *y* to *i* and add *er*.	Put *more* before adjectives with three or more syllables. Put *more* before *modern* and *spacious*.

PRACTICE

Compare the apartments. Fill in the blanks with the correct comparative form.

1. (large) The apartment in Brooklyn is _____ *larger* _____ than the apartment in Queens.

2. (new) The kitchen is _____.

3. (sunny) It's on the top floor, so it's _____ than the apartment in Queens.

4. (noisy) It's on a _____ street than the apartment in Queens.

5. (close) It's also _____ to transportation.

6. (modern) The building is _____ than the building in Queens.

7. (expensive) The apartment in Brooklyn is _____ than the apartment in Queens.

8. (small) The apartment in Queens is _____ than the apartment in Brooklyn.

9. (beautiful) However, it's _____.

10. (large) The bedroom is _____ than the bedroom in the apartment in Brooklyn.

11. (pretty) The apartment is on a _____ street.

12. (cheap) The apartment in Queens is _____ than the apartment in Brooklyn.

New Word: sunny = having bright sunlight

LYNN IS THE MOST TALKATIVE PERSON I KNOW.

Adjective Superlatives with *-est* **and** *The Most*

Verb *To Be*

Marie is	the oldest	person I know.
John is	the messiest	person I know.
Lynn is	the most talkative	person I know.

-est	**-iest**	**the most**
Note: Add *est* to most one-syllable adjectives.	Add *est* to most two-syllable adjectives ending in *y*. Change the *y* to *i* and add *est*.	Put *the most* before adjectives with three or more syllables. Put *the most* before two-syllable adjectives ending in *ed*: *the most* organized.

irregular form: good → best

PRACTICE

Make a superlative sentence about someone you know.

1. nice   _Becky is the nicest person I know._

2. organized   _____

3. busy   _____

4. good singer   _____

5. funny   _____

6. serious   _____

7. old   _____

8. messy   _____

9. intelligent   _____

10. rich   _____

11. beautiful   _____

12. heavy   _____

13. tall   _____

14. talkative   _____

15. good musician   _____

16. strong   _____

A MONKEY IS THE MOST INTELLIGENT.

Review: Adjective Comparatives and Superlatives

Verb *To Be*

A turtle is **slower than** an ant, but a snail is **the slowest** of the three.

Note: When you are comparing two things, add *er* to adjectives or put *more* before adjectives. When you are comparing three or more things, add *est* to adjectives or put *the most* before adjectives.

PRACTICE

Make comparative and superlative sentences about the following animals.

1. intelligent: a dog   a horse   a monkey

   A dog is more intelligent than a horse, but a monkey is the most intelligent of the three.

2. big: a dog   a cat   a horse

   _____

   _____

3. dangerous: a scorpion   a snake   a shark

   _____

   _____

4. strong: a dog   a cat   a horse

   _____

   _____

5. graceful: a cat   a dog   a bird

   _____

   _____

6. fast: a dog   a cat   a horse

   _____

   _____

7. colorful: a butterfly   a goldfish   a parrot

   _____

   _____

8. small: a snail   a mouse   an ant

   _____

   _____

CAROL TAKES MESSAGES MORE CAREFULLY THAN JERRY.

Adverb Comparatives with *-er* and *More*

Simple Present

Carol	Jerry
types 30 words per minute	types 50 words per minute
takes shorthand 90 words per minute	takes shorthand 110 words per minute
answers the telephone very politely	answers the telephone politely
takes messages very carefully	takes messages carefully
spells accurately	spells very accurately
gets to work very early	gets to work early
stays at work late	stays at work very late
works very hard	works hard
finishes her work quickly	finishes his work very quickly
follows directions very carefully	follows directions carefully
dresses very neatly	dresses neatly
gets along with people easily	gets along with people very easily

New Words: shorthand = rapid writing where short forms are used for words and phrases

raise = an increase in salary

CAROL TAKES MESSAGES MORE CAREFULLY THAN JERRY.

Carol takes messages | more carefully than | Jerry.

-er

fast → fast | er |

late → late | r |

Note: Add *r* or *er* to
   one-syllable adverbs.

   irregular form: well → better

more

slowly → | more slowly |

politely → | more politely |

Put *more* before adverbs
with two or more syllables.

exception: early → earlier

PRACTICE

Look at page 114. Then compare Carol's qualities as a secretary with
Jerry's qualities.

1. Jerry *types faster than Carol.*
2. Jerry _____
3. Carol _____
4. _____
5. _____
6. _____
7. _____
8. _____
9. _____
10. _____
11. _____
12. _____

MAKE IT WORK

Both Carol and Jerry want a raise. Tell which person deserves a raise.

_____ deserves a raise because _____
_____
_____
_____

BARBARA WORKS THE HARDEST.

Adverb Superlatives with *-est* and *The Most*

Simple Present

Barbara	Mark	Bill
gets to work very early	gets to work on time	gets to work late
stays at work late	stays at work very late	stays at work late
lives close to the office	lives very close to the office	lives close to the office
dresses neatly	dresses neatly	dresses very neatly
works very carefully	works carefully	works carefully
works quickly	works quickly	works very quickly
works very well under pressure	works well under pressure	works well under pressure
gets along with people very easily	gets along with people easily	gets along with people easily
talks to customers politely	talks to customers politely	talks to customers very politely
works very hard	works hard	works hard

New Words: under pressure = a situation where something has to be done in a hurry

promotion = an advancement in position

BARBARA WORKS THE HARDEST.

Barbara works the hardest.

-est	**the most**
hard → hard est	neatly → the most neatly
	carefully → the most carefully
Note: Add *est* to one-syllable regular adverbs.	Put *most* before adverbs with two or more syllables.
irregular forms: well → best	exception: early → earliest

PRACTICE

Look at page 116. Then tell about Barbara, Mark, and Bill's qualities as employees.

1. Barbara _gets to work the earliest._
2. Mark _____
3. _____
4. _____
5. _____
6. _____
7. _____
8. _____
9. _____
10. _____

MAKE IT WORK

All three employees want a promotion. The boss doesn't want to promote Barbara because she's a woman. Tell the boss why Barbara deserves a promotion.

Barbara deserves a promotion because _____
_____
_____
_____

ALBERTA HAS MORE FRIENDS THAN OLGA.

Review: Comparisons with Adjectives, Adverbs and Nouns

Verb *To Be*, Simple Present

> Alberta is heavier than Olga.
>
> She plays tennis better than Olga.
>
> She has more friends than Olga.

PRACTICE

Compare Alberta and Olga. Begin your sentences with *Alberta*.

1. Alberta is 115 pounds, and Olga is 105 pounds.

   Alberta is heavier than Olga.

2. Alberta is 5 feet 2 inches tall. Olga is 5 feet 4 inches tall.

   _____

3. Alberta is 30 years old. Olga is 27 years old.

   _____

4. Alberta dresses neatly, but Olga doesn't always dress neatly.

   _____

5. Alberta has a lot of friends. Olga has only a few friends.

   _____

6. Alberta is very pretty. Olga is pretty.

   _____

7. Alberta plays tennis very well. Olga plays tennis well.

   _____

8. Alberta reads very quickly. Olga reads quickly.

   _____

9. Alberta is very intelligent. Olga is intelligent.

   _____

10. Alberta makes $40,000 a year. Olga makes $50,000 a year.

    _____

I DON'T KNOW WHAT SHE NEEDS.

Noun Clauses as Objects

Verb *To Be*, Simple Present

What does she need?	I don't know what she needs.
What's her favorite color?	I don't know what her favorite color is.

PRACTICE

Answer the questions. Begin with *I don't know.*

1. It's Louise's birthday. What can we get her?

   I don't know what we can get her.

2. What does she need?

   _____

3. What does she want?

   _____

4. What's her favorite color?

   _____

5. What kind of book does she like?

   _____

6. What type of jewelry does she like?

   _____

7. What size glove does she wear?

   _____

8. What's her favorite perfume?

   _____

9. What kind of candy does she like?

   _____

10. What's her favorite flower?

    _____

MAKE IT WORK

Answer the question. What size blouse does your mother wear?

_____

I DON'T KNOW WHERE IT'S LOCATED.

Noun Clauses as Objects

Simple Present, Simple Past

What's the name of this statue?

I don't know | what the name of the statue is. | OR

It's the Statue of Liberty.

Note: Do not contract words with *is* at the end of a sentence

irregular past tense verb: cost → cost

PRACTICE

Answer the questions. Begin with *I don't know.*

1   What's the name of the statue above?

I don't know what the name of the statue is.

2. Where is it located?

3. What does it represent?

4. How old is it?

5. Where did it come from?

6. How did it get to the United States?

7. How much did it cost?

8. How high is it?

9.   What's it made of?

10. What is the statue holding?

MAKE IT WORK

Check your answers. Then tell a classmate about the Statue of Liberty.

New Word: represent = be a sign or symbol of

DO YOU KNOW HOW LONG IT IS?

Noun Clauses as Objects

Verb *To Be*, Simple Present, Present Continuous

How long is it?

Do you know | how long   it is?

PRACTICE

You and your friend want to go to a new movie. Ask your friend questions about the movie. Begin with *Do you know.*

1. What's the name of the movie?

   Do you know what the name of the movie is?

2. What is it about?

   _____

3. What time does it start?

   _____

4. What time does it end?

   _____

5. How long is it?

   _____

6. Where is it playing?

   _____

7. Where's the Strand Theater?

   _____

8. How far is it?

   _____

9. How long does it take to get there?

   _____

10. How much does the movie cost?

    _____

MAKE IT WORK

A new restaurant just opened in your area. A friend has invited you to go there with him. Ask him one question about the restaurant.

_____

WOULD YOU PLEASE TELL HIM TO CALL ME?

Object Pronoun Reference

Simple Present, Future with _Will_, Polite Imperatives

■ Is John there?

☐ No, he isn't.

■ Would you please tell him to call me ?

nouns	subject pronouns	object pronouns
	I	me
	you	you
John	he	him
Susan Burns	she	her
the telephone number	it	it
Mr. and Mrs. Burns	they	them

PRACTICE

Fill in the dialogues with the correct object pronouns.

■ Is Susan Burns there? ☐ She's at a meeting. May I give _her_ a message?
  (1)

■ Yes. This is Leonard Peterson. Would you ask _____ to call _____ before
  (2)   (3)

noon? ☐ Does she have your phone number?

■ Yes, I think she has _____ , but it's 555-2323.
  (4)

■ Are your parents at home? ☐ No, they aren't. Who's calling?

■ My name is John B. Goode, but they don't know _____. I'm a
  (5)

photographer. Please tell _____ I called. I'll call _____ tomorrow.
  (6)   (7)

■ May I speak to Dr. Lau? ☐ He's with a patient right now. May I give

_____ a message?
  (8)

■ This is Dennis Mason. Would you please tell _____ to call _____ right
  (9)   (10)

away? It's very important. My number is 555-0372. ☐ I'll tell _____. I'm
  (11)

sure he'll call _____ this afternoon.
  (12)

SHE WORKS WITH ME.

Object vs. Subject Pronouns

Simple Present

subject pronouns		object pronouns
I	know	her.
She	works with	me.

PRACTICE

Circle the correct answer.

1. ■ Do you know   she / (her) ?

2. □ Yes, I know   she / her.   She works with   I / me.

3. ■ What does   she / her   do?

4. □ She / Her   works in the office.

5. ■ Is   she / her   married?

6. □ No,   she / her   is divorced.

7. ■ How old is   she / her ?

8. □ I don't know. Why are you asking so many questions about   she / her?

9. ■ Because I want to ask   she / her   for a date!

MAKE IT WORK

Correct Florie and Marie's English. Rewrite the dialogue.

Florie: Do you want to go to a movie with Bob and I?
Marie: No, thanks. John and me are going to watch television tonight.

Florie: _____

Marie: _____

New Word: date = an appointment with a person for a social event

THEY'LL HELP THEMSELVES WHEN THEY GET HUNGRY.

Reflexive Pronouns

Simple Present, Future with _Will_

	singular		plural
I'll enjoy	myself.	We'll enjoy	ourselves.
You'll enjoy	yourself.	We'll enjoy	yourselves.
He'll enjoy	himself.	They'll enjoy	themselves.
She'll enjoy	herself.		

Note: Reflexive pronouns refer back to the subject of the sentence.
by myself, by herself, and so on = _alone_

PRACTICE

Fill in the dialogue with the correct reflexive pronouns.

Babysitter: Hi, I'm the baby sitter.

Mrs. Taylor: Hello. Please come in. Make ___yourself___ at home. There's lots of
(1)

food in the refrigerator. Please help _____.
(2)

Babysitter: Don't worry about me. I'll fix _____ something to eat.
(3)

What do the children like to eat?

Mrs. Taylor: They'll help _____ when they get hungry. Oh, and don't
(4)

let Greg to climb any trees. He sometimes hurts _____.
(5)

Watch Melissa. She shouldn't be by _____. Yesterday she
(6)

burned _____ on the stove.
(7)

Babysitter: Don't worry. I'll watch her. What do the children like to do?

Mrs. Taylor: Oh, they'll amuse _____. And there's one more thing. Jeff
(9)

can't play with his knife. I don't want him to cut _____.
(8)

Call us if the children don't behave_____. The number is
(10)

555-3306.

New Words: amuse = spend time in a pleasant way   behave = act in a proper
manner

124

SHE DID IT HERSELF.

Reflexive Pronouns

Simple Present, Simple Past, Future with _Will_

singular		plural	
I did it	myself.	We did it	ourselves.
You did it	yourself.	You did it	yourselves.
He did it	himself.	They did it	themselves.
She did it	herself.		

irregular past tense verb: build → built

PRACTICE

Fill in the blanks with the correct reflexive pronouns.

Lucy and Sandro bought an old house in Missouri. The house needed a lot

of work. They didn't have a lot of money, so they decided to do most of the

work _themselves_ . People told them that they could never redo the kitchen
(1)

_____. "But," said Lucy, "we read lots of do-it-yourself books, and
(2)

then we began. Slowly we learned to do everything _____."
(3)

Sandro put in new kitchen cabinets, which he built _____. "It's
(4)

much cheaper if you do it _____, and you can save _____
(5) (6)

thousands of dollars." Lucy painted the entire kitchen _____. She also
(7)

made the kitchen curtains _____. "I enjoyed doing it _____,"
(8) (9)

said Lucy. "Next year we hope to add a family room to the house. Of course,

we'll do all of the work _____."
(10)

MAKE IT WORK

Name something you made or built yourself.

_____

New Words: redo = do again   refinish = put a new surface on

FOUR TIES ARE MADE OF SILK. THE OTHER IS MADE OF COTTON.

Another, The Other, and The Others

Verb To Be

One tie is made of cotton.
| The other ties | are made of silk.
| The others | are made of silk.

Four ties are made of silk.
| The other tie | is made of cotton.
| The other | is made of cotton.

Two ties are $12.95.
| Another tie | is $15.50.
| Another | is $17.95.

Note: the others = the only ones left (plural)
　　　the other = the only one left (singular)
　　　another = one of several (singular)

P R A C T I C E

Look at the picture above. Then fill in the blanks with *another, the other,* or *the others.* Use the word *tie* or *ties* when necessary.

Two ties are less than $15.50.

1. ____*The*____ ____*other*____ ____*ties*____ are more than $15.50.

2. ____*The*____ ____*others*____ are more than $15.50.

Two ties are $12.95.

3. _____ _____ is $16. 95.

4. _____ is $17. 95.

Four ties need to be dry-cleaned.

5. _____ _____ _____ is washable.

6. _____ _____ is washable.

Two ties are narrow.

7. _____ _____ _____ are wide.

8. _____ _____ are wide.

One tie is striped.

9. _____ _____ is plaid.

10. _____ is plaid.

THE OTHERS ARE TALL.

Another, The Other, and The Others

Simple Present, Present Continuous

One woman is short.	**The others** are tall.
Four women are tall.	**The other** is short.
Three women are wearing dresses.	**Another** is wearing a suit.

Note: *The others* is plural. *Another* and *the other* are singular.
another = one of several   the other = the only one left

PRACTICE

Look at the picture below. Then fill in the blanks with *another, the other*, or *the others*.

1. One woman is short. _____*The others*_____ are tall.

2. Four women are thin. _____ is fat.

3. One woman is fat. _____ are thin.

4. Four women are middle-aged. _____ is young.

5. Three women are wearing dresses. _____ is wearing a suit.

6. Four women have short hair. _____ has long hair.

7. One woman has a hat on. _____ don't have hats on.

8. Two women have high heels on. _____ has boots on.

9. One woman isn't smiling. _____ are smiling.

10. Four women are talking. _____ is looking at her watch.

I LIKE LIVING WITH OTHER PEOPLE, BUT I DON'T MIND LIVING BY MYSELF.

Review: Reflexives, *Other, Another,*

Simple Present

I like working by [myself,]   but I don't mind working with [other people.]

I like working with [other people,] but I don't mind working by [myself.]

I like working with [another person.]

Note: You can use the infinitive or the gerund after the verb *like.*

PRACTICE

Which of the activities below do you like doing by yourself? Which activities do you like doing with other people or another person? Look at the examples above. Then write sentences about yourself.

1. (work)   *I like working by myself, but I don't mind working*

                  with other people.   OR   I like working by myself.

2. (live)   _____

                  _____

3. (take a vacation) _____

                  _____

4. (go to the movies) _____

                  _____

5. (eat at a restaurant) _____

                  _____

6. (take a walk) _____

                  _____

7. (listen to music) _____

                  _____

8. (go shopping) _____

                  _____

9. (read)   _____

                  _____

10. (watch TV)   _____

                  _____

SHE SENT HOLIDAY CARDS TO HER FRIENDS.

To, For, or No Preposition with Indirect Objects

Simple Past

> **objects**
>
> **indirect**   **direct**   **indirect**
>
> Barbara Ann sent her friends holiday cards.
>
> She sent   holiday cards | to | her friends.
>
> Note: Use *to* or *for* when the indirect object comes after the direct object.
>   Do not use *to* or *for* when the indirect object comes first.
>
>   Use *to* after the verbs below.
>   send   mail   give   serve   write
>
>   Use *for* after the verbs below.
>   buy   get   make   bake   cook

PRACTICE

Fill in the blanks with *to*, *for*, or a line (—) for nothing.

1. Barbara Ann sent _____—_____ her friends holiday cards.

2. She wrote letters _____ some friends.

3. She mailed a gift _____ her grandmother.

4. She also mailed _____ her grandfather a gift.

5. She bought _____ her mother a blouse.

6. She bought perfume _____ her older sister.

7. She made an apron _____ her younger sister.

8. She got _____ her children toys.

9. She also got clothes _____ them.

10. She gave a book _____ her father.

11. She baked some cookies _____ her aunt and uncle.

12. She gave _____ her husband a tie.

13. She cooked a big meal _____ everyone.

14. She served turkey _____ everyone.

15. Afterwards, she served _____ everyone dessert.

MOST MEN ARE INTERESTED IN SPORTS.

Adjective + Preposition

Verb *To Be*

Most men are interested **in** sports.		
Most women are bored **by** sports.		

by	**in**	**of**
bored	interested	tired
entertained		frightened
fascinated		
shocked		

P R A C T I C E

Look at the chart below. Then make sentences you believe are true.

		interested		sports.
		frightened		the latest fashions.
		bored	by	violent movies.
Most people	are	fascinated	in	TV commercials.
Most men		entertained	of	the news on TV.
Most women		tired		sharks.
		shocked		snakes.
				their jobs.
				cars.

1. *Most men are interested in sports.* _____

2. _____

3. _____

4. _____

5. _____

6. _____

7. _____

8. _____

9. _____

10. _____

11. _____

12. _____

YOU SHOULD CALL HIM BACK WITHIN A DAY OR TWO.

Separable Two-Word Verbs

Should, Have To

If it's cold, you should turn	noun or pronoun object	particle	noun object only
		on	the heat.
	the heat	on.	
	it	on.	

Note: Use an object pronoun before the particle, *not* after the particle.

two-word verbs

take off = remove	call up = telephone
take back = return	✔ call back = return a telephone call
turn down = lower	fill up = make full
turn off = shut off	fill out = complete
turn on = start	start up = cause a motor to begin

PRACTICE

Fill in the blanks with a pronoun and a two-word verb from the list above.

1. If you get a message to return someone's phone call, you should
   _____call_____ ___him (or her)___ _____back_____ within a day or two.

2. If you are in a movie theater and the sound is loud, you should ask the
   manager to _____ _____ _____.

3. If you buy an appliance that doesn't work, you should _____
   _____ _____ to the store.

4. Before you take a bath in a bathtub, you should _____
   _____ _____ with water before you get in.

5. When a man with a hat enters a room, he should _____
   _____ _____.

6. You shouldn't leave any appliances on when you aren't at home. You
   should _____ _____ _____ before you leave the house.

7. If you want to cancel an appointment with a doctor, you should
   _____ _____ _____ 24 hours in advance.

8. If you want a job, you have to get an application and then _____
   _____ _____.

I LOOKED THEM UP.

Separable Two-Word Verbs

Simple Past

> Look up the new words.
>
> I looked them up.
>
> Note: Use an object pronoun before the particle, *not* after the particle.
>
> Common particles are *up, down, in, on, over, out, off.*
>
> **two-word verbs**
>
> look over = examine   read over = read again
>   look up = search for information   fill in = write information in spaces

PRACTICE

Put the object pronouns before the particles. Use *I* and the past tense.

1. Turn on the light.   *I turned it on.*

2. Put on your glasses.   _____

3. Pick up a pen.   _____

4. Look over the homework.   _____

5. Write down your answers.   _____

6. Fill in the blanks.   _____

7. Look up the new words
   in the dictionary.   _____
                                 _____

8. Read over your paper.   _____

9. Cross out your mistakes.   _____

10. Hand in the homework.   _____

MAKE IT WORK

Fill in the blanks. You can use negative or affirmative verbs.

I did a homework assignment on _____.

I _____ the homework assignment before I begin to write.

I _____ my answers _____.

I _____ the homework assignment _____ on time.

IT'S THE FIRST HOUSE ON THE RIGHT.

Review: Prepositions of Place: *In, On, At*

Verb *To Be*, **Simple Present**

I live in an apartment.	I live on Royal Lane.
in Dallas.	on the corner of Royal Lane and High Street.
in Room 532.	on the right side of the street.
in the basement.	on the top floor.
I live at 56 Royal Lane.	

PRACTICE

Fill in the blanks with *in, on,* or *at.*

1. I live ___*on*___ Royal Lane ___*in*___ North Dallas.

2. It's the first house _____ the right.

3. I live _____ 52 Main Street.

4. That's _____ Houston.

5. I live _____ apartment 63-C.

6. It's the third building _____ the left.

7. I live _____ the basement of the building.

8. My address is 412 High Street _____ Dallas.

9. I work _____ the top floor _____ Room 6.

10. I work _____ Silverton _____ the corner of Union and Fourth.

11. I live _____ 16 Park Place, apartment 1-B.

12. It's the second door _____ your right.

MAKE IT WORK

Read the telephone message. Then write a report of a fire in your kitchen.

This is an emergency!	This is _____
There's a robber in my apartment!	There's _____
I live at 2559 High Street in Dallas	_____
in apartment 5-A.	_____
Please come immediately!	_____

New Word: emergency = an unexpected event that you must do something
about at once

133

SHE'S WORKED FOR ME SINCE MARCH.

Review: Prepositions of Time: *In, At, For, Since, From-To*

Simple Past, Present Perfect, Present Perfect Continuous

She worked		
	on	Saturday.
	on	February 1st.
	at	night.
	from	9:00 **to** 5:00. (a beginning time and an ending time)
She worked for me	for	two months. (a period of time)
	since	March. (a beginning of time)

PRACTICE

Fill in the blanks with *on, at, from, to, for,* or *since.*

MEMO

To: Nancy Ping, Personnel Manager
From: Barbara Woods, Art Director
Re: Mary Hee Kim

   Mary Hee Kim has been working for this company (1.) _since_ 1990.
She has been working in the art department (2.) _____ 1992. She has
been working directly with me (3.) _____ two months now. She came
to the art department (4.) _____ March 15th. She has been working on
a special project (5.) _____ April. She hasn't missed a day of work
(6.) _____ a year. Last month, she worked extra hours to get her work
done on time. She came into the office (7.) _____ 8:00 A.M.
(8.) _____ Saturday. She worked (9.) _____ 8:00 _____ 6:00.
She also worked (10.) _____ night (11.) _____ April 3rd and 4th.
   Mary hasn't received a raise (12.) _____ three years. I recommend
that she receive a raise.

MAKE IT WORK

Fill in the blanks if you work. Use *for* or *since.*

I've been working at my present job _____.

I've been working in the same department _____.

I haven't received a raise _____.

APPENDIX

Irregular Verbs

Simple Form	Past Form	Past Participle
be	was/were	been
become	became	become
begin	begin	begun
break	broke	broken
bring	brought	brought
build	built	built
buy	bought	bought
catch	caught	caught
come	came	come
cost	cost	cost
cut	cut	cut
do	did	done
drink	drank	drunk
drive	drove	driven
eat	ate	eaten
fall	fell	fallen
feed	fed	fed
find	found	found
fly	flew	flown
get	got	gotten
give	gave	given
go	went	gone
grow	grew	grown
have	had	had
hear	heard	heard
hit	hit	hit
hurt	hurt	hurt
know	knew	known
leave	left	left
make	made	made
meet	met	met
pay	paid	paid
put	put	put
quit	quit	quit
read	read	read
ride	rode	ridden
ring	rang	rung
run	ran	run
say	said	said
see	saw	seen
sell	sold	sold
send	sent	sent

Irregular Verbs

Simple Form	Past Form	Past Participle
sleep	slept	slept
speak	spoke	spoken
steal	stole	stolen
swim	swam	swum
take	took	taken
teach	taught	taught
tear	tore	torn
tell	told	told
throw	threw	thrown
wear	wore	worn
write	wrote	written

Irregular Noun Plurals

Singular	Plural
child	children
deer	deer
fish	fish
foot	feet
goose	geese
mouse	mice
person	people
sheep	sheep

Uncountable Nouns

air	heat	snow
air pollution	industry	spinach
alcohol	jewelry	sugar
beer	juice	tea
bread	lightning	traffic
broccoli	litter	transportation
candy	mail	trash
cake	meat	water
champagne	medicine	weather
cheese	milk	wine
coffee	money	work
corn	music	yogurt
crime	noise	
dust	perfume	
electricity	rain	
food	smog	
gasoline	smoke	
grass		

* Some of these words are occasionally used as countable nouns.

ANSWERS TO EXERCISES

Page 1
2. baths
3. bedrooms
4. walls
5. roofs
6. patios
7. garages
8. fireplaces
9. dens
10. studies
11. bookshelves
12. ovens
13. window boxes
14. radios
15. floors

Page 2 and 3
2. Goldfish aren't dangerous.
3. Rattlesnakes are dangerous.
4. Deer aren't dangerous.
5. Geese aren't dangerous.
6. Rats are (aren't) dangerous.
7. Alligators are dangerous.
8. Wasps aren't (are) dangerous.
9. Butterflies aren't dangerous.
10. Sheep aren't dangerous.
11. Scorpions are dangerous.
12. Mice aren't dangerous.

Make It Work
Individual answers. Some possible answers are:
I'm afraid of sharks.
I'm afraid of alligators (snakes).

Pages 4 and 5
Individual answers.

Pages 6
2. the picture frames
3. the rose bushes
4. the garden tools
5. the beach towels
6. the paint brushes
7. the salad bowls
8. the coffee tables
9. the shower curtains
10. the rubber gloves
11. the wine glasses
12. the wall clocks

Make It Work
They're birthday cards.

Page 7
2. A shark is a fish.
3. A snake is a reptile.
4. A butterfly is an insect.
5. A goose is a bird.
6. An alligator is a reptile.
7. A wasp is an insect.
8. A parrot is a bird.
9. A mouse is a rodent.
10. A fly is an insect.
11. A turtle is a reptile.
12. A cockroach is an insect.
13. A rat is a rodent.
14. An ant is an insect.
15. A goldfish is a fish.

Make It Work
Individual answers. Answers that match the pictures are:
a parrot
a butterfly
a goldfish

Pages 8 and 9
2. The, the
3. The, —
4. The, —
5. The, —
6. —, the
7. —, the
8. —, —, —,
9. —, —
10. The, —
11. The, —, —
12. The, the
13. —, the, the
14. —, —
15. —, —, the

Page 10
2. a, the
3. the, The
4. the, a
5. a, the
6. the, a
7. the, The
8. the, a
9. the, The, the
10. the, the
11. the, the
12. The, a
13. the, the
14. the

Page 11
2. Waikiki is a beach.
3. South America is a continent.
4. The Pacific is an ocean.
5. An apple is a fruit.
6. Corn is a vegetable.
7. The Nile is a river.
8. A shark is a fish.
9. An ant is an insect.
10. Puerto Rico is an island.
11. The Netherlands is a country.
12. Coffee is a beverage.

Pages 12 and 13
2. He's 48 (years old).
3. He's 5' 8" (five feet, eight inches tall).
4. He weighs 180 pounds (LBS).
5. He has blond hair. (His hair is blond.)
6. He has blue eyes. (His eyes are blue.)
7. He doesn't smoke. (He's a non-smoker.)
8. He's a teacher.
9. He makes (earns) over $30,000 a year.
10. He's single. (He isn't married.)
11. He speaks English and French.
12. He plays (enjoys/likes) tennis and ping pong.
13. He likes reading (to read). (His hobby is reading.)

Page 14
Individual questions.

Page 15
2. gets
3. clean
4. cleans
5. fix
6. fixes
7. answer
8. answers
9. get
10. helps
11. answer
12. answers
13. drive
14. drives

Pages 16 and 17
2. decided
3. baked
4. packed
5. walked
6. jumped
7. followed
8. asked
9. answered
10. liked
11. arrived
12. noticed
13. entered
14. looked
15. killed

Page 18
2. live
3. visit
4. live
5. walked
6. jumped
7. followed
8. stop
9. talk

10. asked
11. want
12. like
13. liked
14. walked
15. see
16. expected
17. reached
18. pulled
19. kill
20. killed

Make It Work
There isn't any (left).
There aren't any

Page 19
Individual answers. See the Appendix for irregular verbs.

Page 20 and 21
2. She attended Huntington Elementary School from 1960 to 1968.
3. She attended Huntington Elementary School for eight years.
4. She completed the eighth (8th) grade.
5. She attended high school for four years.
6. She went to Newport High School.
7. She attended Newport High School from 1969 to 1973.
8. She completed the twelfth (12th) grade.
9. She received a diploma.
10. She graduated from Newport High School.
11. She went to the University of California.
12. Her major subject was English.
13. She attended the University of California from 1974 to 1978.
14. She received a bachelor's degree.

Pages 22 and 23
2. He was an English teacher.
3. He taught English.
4. He worked for Greenfield High School for eleven years.

5. He earned $27,500 (a year).
6. He left Greenfield High School because he got a job in California.
7. He worked at Ames Department Store.
8. He was a sales clerk.
9. He sold furniture.
10. He worked for Ames Department Store for two years.
11. He earned $10,400 (a year).
12. He left Ames Department Store because he got a teaching job in Massachusetts.

Page 24
2. (How long) did you work for Star Shoe Company?
3. (Who) did you work for?
4. (When) did she leave A. B.C. Company?
5. (Why) did she leave A.B.C. Company?
6. (When) did you graduate from college?
7. (What college) did you graduate from?
8. (Where) did he attend high school?
9. (When) did he attend high school?
10. (What) high school did he attend?
11. (How long) did she work for National Bank?
12. (Who) did she work for?
13. (How much) did he earn at Selby Company?
14. (What) did you teach at Harbor High School?
15. (When) did you teach at Harbor High School?
16. (How long) did you teach at Harbor High School?

Pages 25
2. She mailed her grandmother a gift.
3. She bought her mother a blouse.
4. She got her children toys.
5. She gave her father a book.

6. She made her sister an apron.
7. She baked her aunt and uncle cookies.
8. She got her husband a tie.
9. She cooked her family a big meal.
10. She served everyone turkey.

Page 26
2. The waiter brought some wine to them.
3. He poured some wine for Mr. Green and Mr. Bang.
4. Then the waiter handed menus to them.
5. Mr. Green gave their order to the waiter.
6. He ordered steak for them.
7. After fifteen minutes the waiter served their food to them.
8. When the meal was over, the waiter handed the check to Mr. Green.
9. Mr. Green gave some money to the waiter.
10. He also left a tip for the waiter.

Page 27
3. for
4. —
5. for
6. —
7. to
8. to
9. for
10. —
11. to
12. to
13. —
14. for

Page 28
2. screamed
3. started
4. saw
5. chased
6. ran
7. hit
8. came
9. heard
10. began
11. joined
12. caught
13. found
14. heard
15. called

Pages 29 and 30
2. playing
3. practicing
4. doing
5. practicing
6. to give
7. getting
8. to have
9. to have
10. staying
11. being
12. to own
13. to buy
14. driving
15. seeing
16. working
17. to support
18. to be

Page 31

2. to have
3. retiring
4. working, to do
5. being
6. working
7. swimming, gardening
8. doing
9. writing, to take
10. to travel

Page 32

2. to buy
3. looking (to look)
4. dancing
5. dancing
6. to dance
7. to learn
8. smoking
9. jogging
10. swimming
11. being
12. fishing
13. camping
14. fishing
15. camping
16. to go

Page 34

2. to take
3. working
4. to go
5. working
6. to work
7. working
8. to be
9. having
10. to give
11. staying
12. to be

Page 35

2. made
3. did
4. did
5. did
6. did
7. made
8. made
9. did
10. do
11. did
12. did
13. do
14. made
15. did

Page 36

Individual answers.

Page 37

Individual answers beginning with *I'll probably*.

Page 38

2. will look, walks
3. is, will leave
4. will take, leave
5. leave, will throw
6. arrive, will drink
7. dance, will dance
8. will throw, leave
9. will be
10. throws, will get

Page 39

2. After she sees London, she'll fly to Paris.
3. When she's in Paris, she'll see the Eiffel Tower.
4. After she leaves Paris, she'll go to Rome.
5. When she visits Rome, she'll go to some museums.
6. When she's in Rome, she'll see some famous fountains.
7. After she sees Rome, she'll go to Madrid.
8. After she spends a day in Madrid, she'll go to Athens.
9. When she visits Athens, she'll see some famous statues.
10. After she leaves Athens, she'll fly back to Tokyo.

Page 40

Individual answers beginning with *If it* and including *I'll* or *I won't*.

Page 41

Individual answers beginning with *I'd* or *I wouldn't*.

Page 42

Individual answers beginning with *If I were....*

Page 43

Individual answers. Some possible answers are:

2. If I needed money, I'd call my father (a friend).
3. If I had a headache, I'd take some aspirin.
4. If I felt sick, I'd go to bed.
5. If I broke my arm, I'd call a doctor (the hospital).
6. If my house were on fire, I'd call the fire department.
7. If I saw a car accident, I'd call an ambulance (the police/the police department).
8. If someone robbed my house (apartment), I'd call the police (the police department).
9. If I lost the keys to my house (apartment), I'd call my husband (wife). (I'd climb in through the window.)
10. If someone stole my wallet, I'd call the police (the police department).

Page 44

Individual answers.

Pages 45 and 46

2. 'm teaching
3. 's going
4. is writing
5. ('s not) isn't working
6. are building
7. 're doing
8. 're working
9. 's studying
10. 's getting
11. is going
12. 're living
13. 're working
14. is building
15. is selling
16. are living
17. ('re not) aren't doing
18. isn't working
19. is looking
20. 're getting

Page 47

2. He's flying on American (Airlines).
3. He's stopping in Chicago for an hour.
4. He's changing planes in Chicago.
5. He's flying on United (Airlines).
6. He's arriving in New York at 6:38 p.m.
7. He's staying in New York for three days.
8. He's returning to Seattle on July 2nd.
9. He's leaving at 12:50 p.m.

10. He's flying directly to Seattle.
11. He's flying on TWA.
12. He's arriving in Seattle at 9:20 p.m.

Page 48
2. was making
3. was cleaning
4. were jogging
5. were playing
6. was working
7. were sleeping
8. was listening
9. were studying
10. was watching
11. were exercising
12. was taking
13. were eating
14. was using

Page 49
2. He was talking on the telephone when the accident happened.
3. He was watching television when Steve came over.
4. He was relaxing on the patio when it began to rain.
5. He was cooking dinner when the baby started to cry.
6. He was eating dinner when he heard a loud noise.
7. He was studying when the doorbell rang.
8. He was taking a bath when Mary called.
9. He was reading a book when the dog started to bark.
10. He was taking a nap when his alarm clock went off.

Page 50
2. She hurt her back while she was moving furniture.
3. He cut his finger while he was cooking.
4. I fell down while I was riding a bicycle.
5. He slipped while he was walking in the snow.
6. She bumped her head while she was getting out of the car.

7. He tore his pants while he was working in the yard.
8. I burned my hand while I was cooking.
9. They had an accident while they were driving.
10. He broke his leg while he was playing football.

Page 51
2. cut, was shaving
3. was taking, rang
4. was taking, slipped, fell
5. rang, was making
6. was talking, began
7. was making, knocked
8. was frying, burned
9. broke, was doing
10. decided, went

Pages 52 and 53
2. They've been typing since 12:00.
3. He's been looking at the bulletin board since 1:45.
4. She's been talking on the telephone since 1:30.
5. They've been checking figures since 10:00.
6. She's been sitting at the switchboard since 9:00.
7. He's been waiting since 1:20.
8. She's been opening the mail since 1:45.
9. He's been writing a report since 11:00.
10. He's been out to lunch since 11:30.

Page 54
3. No, they haven't.
4. Yes, they have.
5. Yes, she has.
6. No, they haven't.
7. Yes, they have.
8. No, they haven't.
9. No, they haven't.
10. No, he hasn't.
11. Yes, he has.
12. No, she hasn't.
13. Yes, she has.
14. No, he hasn't.
15. Yes, he has.

Page 55
2. How long have you been listening to the boss?
3. How long have you been working on the report?
4. How long has he been talking on the telephone?
5. How long have they been eating lunch?
6. How long has she been sitting at the switchboard?
7. How long have you been waiting in the lobby?
8. How long has he been using the computer?
9. How long have you been filing letters?
10. How long have they been reading the mail?
11. How long has she been standing at the coffee machine?
12. How long have you been typing letters?

Pages 56 and 57
2. She's cooked dinner three times so far.
3. She's vacuumed once so far.
4. She's ironed the clothes once so far.
5. Myra and Becky have changed the beds once so far.
6. Roy has cleaned his room once so far.
7. He's watered the plants twice so far.
8. He's emptied the wastepaper baskets once so far.
9. Becky has dusted the living room once so far.
10. She's cleaned her room once so far.
11. Roy and Becky have cleaned the bathroom once so far.
12. They've washed the dishes four times so far.
13. Bill has cooked dinner once so far.
14. He's carried out the trash once so far.

Page 58

3. for
4. since
5. for
6. since
7. since
8. for
9. since
10. for
11. for
12. since
13. since
14. for
15. since

Page 59

2. He hasn't taken out the trash since Thursday.
3. They haven't cleaned their rooms for two days.
4. She hasn't fed the dog since yesterday.
5. She hasn't washed the clothes for four days.
6. She hasn't ironed the clothes since Wednesday.
7. They haven't done the dishes since yesterday.
8. He hasn't watered the plants since Thursday.
9. He hasn't paid the bills for a month.
10. She hasn't written a letter for two weeks.

Pages 60

2. How many times has she fed the dog today?
3. How many times have they cleaned their rooms this week?
4. How many times has she cooked dinner this week?
5. How many times has he washed the car this month?
6. How many times have they cleaned the bathroom this week?
7. How many times has he taken out the trash this week?
8. How many times has she ironed the clothes this month?
9. How many times have they changed the beds this month?
10. How many times has she dusted the living room this week?

Page 61

2. yet, already
3. yet, yet
4. already, yet
5. already
6. already, yet
7. yet, already
8. already, yet
9. yet
10. yet, already

Make It Work

Individual answers:
I've already had lunch.
I haven't had lunch yet.
I've already had dinner.
I haven't had dinner yet.

Page 62

3. He's already gone to the doctor.
4. He hasn't gone to the bank yet.
5. He hasn't bought traveler's checks yet.
6. He's already gotten travel insurance.
7. He's already made hotel reservations.
8. He hasn't paid for his plane ticket yet.
9. He hasn't picked up his plane ticket yet.
10. He's already gotten a passport.
11. He's already taken his suit to the cleaners.
12. He hasn't packed his suitcase yet.

Page 63

3. Yes, they have.
4. Yes, he has.
5. No, he hasn't.
6. Yes, he has.
7. Yes, he has.
8. Yes, they have.
9. No, he hasn't.
10. No, he hasn't.
11. No, they haven't.
12. No, he hasn't.
13. Yes, he has.
14. No, they haven't.

Make It Work

Individual answers:
Yes, I have.
No, I haven't.

Page 64

2. Have your children seen it yet?
3. Have you read it yet?
4. Has your husband read it yet?
5. Have you met them yet?
6. Has your husband met them yet?
7. Has your son heard it yet?
8. Have you heard it yet?
9. Have you driven on it yet?
10. Has your husband driven on it yet?
11. Have your children seen it yet?
12. Have you seen it yet?

Make It Work

Have you eaten (been/gone) there yet?

Page 65

2. He hasn't been to England.
3. He hasn't been to the Netherlands.
4. He's been to Greece.
5. He hasn't been to Morocco.
6. He hasn't been to Israel.
7. He's been to France.
8. He hasn't been to Germany.
9. He's been to Spain.
10. He hasn't been to the Republic of China.
11. He hasn't been to Japan.
12. He's been to Italy.

Pages 66 and 67

4. 's been
5. works
6. works
7. started
8. 's worked
9. worked
10. worked
11. lived
12. lives
13. 's lived
14. 's lived
15. worked
16. worked
17. lived
18. was
19. lived
20. worked

Pages 68 and 69

2. He was born in Mexico City, Mexico.
3. He lives
4. He's lived in Los Angeles
5. He went to
6. He graduated (received a diploma) from Hollywood High School

7. He's an
8. He's been an assistant television producer
9. He works
10. He's worked for KTLA Television Station
11. He's married. (He has a wife.)
12. He got (was) married
13. He's been married
14. He has
15. He collects (likes to collect)
16. He started to collect (collected)
17. He's collected baseball cards
18. He wants to be (His goal is to be) a TV producer someday.

Pages 70 and 71

2. gone	13. work
3. seen	14. moved
4. been	15. had
5. driven	16. took
6. taken	17. been
7. did	18. been
8. went	19. died
9. lived	20. got
10. wrote	21. am ('m)
11. written	22. have
12. worked	23. had
	24. became

Make It Work

Individual answers in the present perfect beginning with *I've*.

Page 72

3. They've been traveling
4. They've traveled
5. He's written
6. He's been writing
7. They've driven
8. They've been driving
9. She's been cleaning
10. She's cleaned
11. She's been playing
12. She's played

Page 73

2. Could (Would) you turn down the radio? (Would you mind turning down the radio?)
3. Would (Could) you help me with my homework? (Would

you mind helping me with my homework?)
4. Would (Could) you pass (me) the salt?
5. Could (Would) you shut the door? (Would you mind shutting the door on your way out?)
6. Would (Could) you fill it up with regular gas (gasoline)?
7. Would (Could) you drive me to the airport? (Would you mind driving me to the airport?)

Make It Work

Could (Would) you open the door for me? Would you mind signing your name here?)

Page 74

2. You have to answer the phone.
3. You don't have to work at night.
4. You have to work eight hours a day.
5. You don't have to work overtime.
6. You have to work five days a week.
7. You don't have to work on holidays.
8. You don't have to work on Sundays.
9. You have to have experience.
10. You don't have to use a computer.

Page 75

2. A computer programmer has to be able to use a computer.
3. A truck driver has to be able to drive a truck.
4. A cashier has to be able to use a cash register.
5. A barber has to be able to cut hair.
6. An artist has to be able to draw pictures.
7. A musician has to be able to play an instrument.
8. A shoemaker has to be able to fix shoes.
9. A photographer has to be able to take pictures.

10. An airline pilot has to be able to fly a plane.

Page 76

2. They've got to go to class.
3. He's got to mail a letter before 5:00.
4. I've got to go to the bank before 3:00.
5. We've got to get to the wedding on time.
6. She's got to catch the train.
7. He's got to pick up his wife.
8. I've got to leave work early.
9. They've got to be home before dark.
10. You've got to go to bed.

Pages 77 and 78

2. You must not swim
3. You must fasten
4. You must not play
5. You must deposit
6. You must stop.
7. You must not carry (have/take)
8. You must pay
9. You must not enter
10. You must have
11. You must not exit
12. You must not litter

Make It Work

You must not smoke in a theater.
You must have a passport.
You must have a driver (driver's) license.

Page 79

2. don't have to
3. don't have to
4. must not
5. must not
6. don't have to
7. must not
8. don't have to
9. don't have to
10. must not

Page 80

2. You aren't allowed to smoke here.
3. You aren't allowed to fish here.
4. You aren't allowed to ice-skate here.
5. You aren't allowed to litter here.

6. You aren't allowed to play a radio here.
7. You aren't allowed to ride a bicycle here.
8. You aren't allowed to hunt here.
9. You aren't allowed to trespass here.
10. You aren't allowed to camp here.
11. You aren't allowed to park here.
12. You aren't allowed to swim here.

Page 81
3. He'd better not leave his wallet on the counter.
4. He'd better put his wallet away.
5. She'd better not leave the door unlocked.
6. She'd better lock the door.
7. She'd better not walk home late at night.
8. She'd better take a taxi.
9. He'd better not leave his camera in the car.
10. He'd better take his camera with him.
11. She'd better not leave the windows open.
12. She'd better close (lock) the windows.

Page 82
2. You shouldn't be
3. You should wear
4. You should send (bring)
5. You shouldn't be (arrive)
6. You should bring
7. You shouldn't start to eat
8. You shouldn't eat
9. You shouldn't say
10. You should say
11. You should bring (take)
12. You should write (send)

Page 83
2. It might rain tomorrow.
3. It might be warm tomorrow.
4. It will (It'll) be nice (weather) tomorrow.
5. It might be cloudy tomorrow.
6. It will (It'll) probably be windy tomorrow.
7. It might be foggy tomorrow.
8. It might snow tomorrow.
9. It will (It'll) probably be cold tomorrow.
10. It will (It'll) be sunny tomorrow.

Page 84
2. He must be a doctor.
3. She must be a police officer.
4. He must be a painter.
5. He must be a boxer.
6. She must be a waitress.
7. She must be a business executive.
8. He must be a musician.
9. He must be a dancer.
10. He must be a carpenter

Page 85
2. 'd rather eat
3. would rather not eat
4. 'd rather eat
5. 'd rather not cook
6. would rather eat
7. would rather not watch
8. 'd rather go
9. would rather not
10. 'd rather watch

Page 86
Individual answers.
2. Yes, I would. /No, I wouldn't.
3. I'd rather eat French (Italian) food.
4. I'd rather have steak (pizza).
5. No, I wouldn't. /Yes, I would.
6. I'd rather go to a casual (fancy) restaurant.
7. Yes, I would. /No, I wouldn't.
8. I'd rather go somewhere (stay at home).
9. No, I wouldn't. /Yes, I would.
10. I'd rather go to a movie (watch television).

Page 87
Individual answers. Possible answers are given:
2. She should take an umbrella. It might rain.
3. She shouldn't take a lot of clothes. Only one suitcase is allowed.
4. She should take a sweater. It might be cold.
5. She should take a fancy dress. She might need it.
6. She shouldn't take her valuable jewelry. Someone might steal it.
7. She should take a bathing suit. The hotel might have a pool.
8. She should take some walking shoes. She might go for walks.
9. She shouldn't take a fur coat. She won't need it.
10. She should take a scarf. It might be windy.

Pages 88 and 89
3. have to (must) put (deposit)
4. don't have to put (deposit)
5. should take
6. shouldn't keep (try to fix/use)
7. must (have to/'ve got to) smoke
8. must not smoke
9. 'd better study
10. 'd better not go
11. might go
12. might not go
13. must be
14. must not feel

Page 90
2. They had to wash all the windows.
3. They had to put in window screens.
4. They had to fix the stove.
5. They had to buy a refrigerator.
6. They had to build a counter in the kitchen. (They had to build a kitchen counter.)
7. They had to paint the inside of the house.
8. They had to put in light fixtures.

Page 91
2. He didn't have to buy a refrigerator.
3. He didn't have to buy a (new) stove.

4. He didn't have to build a counter in the kitchen.(He didn't have to build a kitchen counter.)
5. He didn't have to paint the inside of the house.
6. He didn't have to fix the roof.
7. He didn't have to put in (new) light fixtures.
8. He didn't have to buy (new) rugs.
9. He didn't have to put in an air conditioner.
10. He didn't have to wash the windows.

Page 92
2. He could play tennis all day
3. He could read without his glasses
4. He could go out every night
5. He could stay up all night
6. He could run up and down the stairs
7. He could lift heavy boxes
8. He could eat rich food
9. He could work for twelve hours a day
10. He could run a mile in fifteen minutes

Pages 93
2. She should have turned off the lights.
3. She should have fed the dog.
4. She should have closed the windows.
5. She should have taken out the trash.
6. She should have made sure the oven was off.
7. She should have turned off the radio.
8. She should have locked all the doors.
9. She should have taken her keys with her.
10. She should have taken her money with her.

Page 94
2. couldn't go
3. had to walk
4. couldn't buy
5. had to buy

6. couldn't use
7. had to take
8. couldn't use
9. had to use
10. couldn't watch
11. couldn't cook
12. had to eat

Page 95
2. is known
3. are grown
4. are covered
5. are picked
6. are packed
7. are delivered
8. are sold
9. are consumed
10. are used
11. are eaten
12. are used

Page 96
2. were hurt
3. were involved
4. was hit
5. were hit
6. were injured
7. was called
8. were notified
9. were notified
10. was put out
11. were taken
12. was closed

Page 97
Shortly after midnight, her house was broken into. The downstairs windows were broken. Her clothes were thrown everywhere. Her jewelry box was unlocked. Her gold jewelry was taken. Her compact disc player and her television were stolen. Some money was taken. The front door was left open. The police were called.

Page 98
2. wasn't interesting.
3. were frightening.
4. was frightened.
5. was confusing.
6. was confused.
7. was shocked.
8. was shocking.

9. was entertained.
10. was entertaining.
11. was fascinating.
12. was fascinated.
13. was surprised.
14. was surprising.

Make It Work
Individual answers. Some possible answers are:
interesting, exciting, entertaining, boring. frightening, surprised, confused, shocked

Page 99
2. bored
3. exciting
4. disappointed
5. boring
6. exhausted
7. amazing
8. amazed
9. terrifying
10. entertaining

Pages 100 and 101
2. There are a lot of antique shops in Lambertville.
3. There are a lot of apartment buildings in Lambertville.
4. There are a few churches in Lambertville.
5. There's a little crime in Lambertville.
6. There are a few grocery stores in Lambertville.
7. There are a few hotels in Lambertville.
8. There's a little industry in Lambertville.
9. There are a few museums in Lambertville.
10. There are a few office buildings in Lambertville.
11. There are a lot of old houses in Lambertville.
12. There are a lot of restaurants in Lambertville.

Page 102
2. There aren't any shops in Titusville.
3. There isn't much traffic in Titusville.
4. There aren't any hotels in Titusville.

144

5. There isn't any industry in Titusville.
6. There aren't many buildings in Titusville.
7. There isn't any litter in Titusville.
8. There aren't any apartments in Titusville.
9. There aren't many houses in Titusville.
10. There aren't any hospitals in Titusville.

Page 103

2.	one	9.	any
3.	no	10.	one
4.	no	11.	no
5.	one	12.	any
6.	any	13.	no
7.	any	14.	any

Page 104

2. My apartment is also too small.
3. The kitchen isn't modern enough.
4. The kitchen is too small.
5. The closets aren't big enough.
6. It isn't close enough to a shopping area.
7. It's too far from the bus station.
8. My street isn't safe enough.
9. The neighborhood is too dangerous.
10. The neighborhood is too noisy.

Page 105

3. She isn't fast enough to run on the track team.
4. She's too slow to run on the track team.
5. He's too young to play professional baseball.
6. He isn't old enough to play professional baseball.
7. He's too small to play on the football team.
8. He isn't big enough to play on the football team.
9. He isn't heavy enough to play on the football team.
10. She isn't good enough to play on the tennis team.
11. She isn't accurate enough to play on the tennis team.
12. She isn't fast enough to play on the tennis team.
13. He's too small to be on the boxing team.
14. He isn't quick enough to be on the boxing team.
15. He isn't strong enough to be on the boxing team.

Page 106

2. I think you learn very quickly.
3. I think you drive very cautiously.
4. I think you read very fast.
5. I think you dress very neatly.
6. I think you dance very gracefully.
7. I think you play tennis very well.
8. I think you listen very attentively.
9. I think you work very hard.
10. I think you swim very well.

Make It Work

Individual answers. Some possible answers are:
I think you sing very well (beautifully). I think you have a nice voice.

Page 107

2. I like it very much.
3. It's very interesting.
4. Are there a lot of students in your class?
5. No, there aren't many students.
6. It's a small class.
7. Are you learning much English?
8. Yes, but I don't speak fast enough.
9. I think you speak English very well.

Page 108

3. You should eat more yogurt.
4. You should eat less sugar.
5. You should eat more carrots.
6. You should drink less alcohol.
7. You should eat fewer potato chips.
8. You should eat less meat.
9. You should drink more milk.
10. You should drink less coffee.
11. You should eat more apples.
12. You should drink fewer soft drinks.
13. You should eat less cheese.
14. You should eat fewer cookies.
15. You should eat more low-fat food.

Page 109

3. The gray cat isn't as heavy as the black cat.
4. The gray cat isn't as long as the black cat.
5. The gray cat isn't as big as the black cat.
6. The gray cat is as gentle as the black cat.
7. The gray cat is as nice as the black cat.
8. The gray cat isn't as beautiful as the black cat.
9. The gray cat is as graceful as the black cat.
10. The gray cat isn't as friendly as the black cat.
11. The gray cat isn't as playful as the black cat.
12. The gray cat is as clean as the black cat.
13. The gray cat isn't as healthy as the black cat.
14. The gray cat is as active as the black cat.

Page 110

2. My gloves are the same as yours.
3. My umbrella is different from yours.
4. My ring is different from yours.
5. My watch is the same as yours.
6. My slacks are the same as yours.
7. My scarf is different from yours.
8. My coat is the same as yours.
9. My shirt is different from yours.

145

10. My wallet is different from yours.

Make It Work

His pants are the same as hers.
His shirt is the same as hers.
His shoes are different from hers.

Page 111

2. newer
3. sunnier
4. noisier
5. closer
6. more modern
7. more expensive
8. smaller
9. more beautiful
10. larger
11. prettier
12. cheaper

Page 112

Individual answers with the following adjective superlatives:

2. Becky is the most organized person I know.
3. Becky is the busiest person I know.
4. Becky is the best singer I know.
5. Becky is the funniest person I know.
6. Becky is the most serious person I know.
7. Becky is the oldest person I know.
8. Becky is the messiest person I know.
9. Becky is the most intelligent person I know.
10. Becky is the richest person I know.
11. Becky is the most beautiful person I know.
12. Becky is the heaviest person I know.
13. Becky is the tallest person I know.
14. Becky is the most talkative person I know.
15. Becky is the best musician I know.
16. Becky is the strongest person I know.

Pages 113

2. A dog is bigger than a cat, but a horse is the biggest of the three.
3. A scorpion is more dangerous than a snake, but a shark is the most dangerous of the three.
4. A dog is stronger than a cat, but a horse is the strongest of the three.
5. A cat is more graceful than a dog, but a bird is the most graceful of the three.
6. A dog is faster than a cat, but a horse is the fastest of the three.
7. A butterfly is more colorful than a goldfish, but a parrot is the most colorful of the three.
8. A snail is smaller than a mouse, but an ant is the smallest of the three.

Page 114 and 115

2. Jerry takes shorthand faster than Carol.
3. Carol answers the telephone more politely than Jerry.
4. Carol takes messages more carefully than Jerry.
5. Jerry spells more accurately than Carol.
6. Carol gets to work earlier than Jerry.
7. Jerry stays at work later than Carol.
8. Carol works harder than Jerry.
9. Jerry finishes his work more quickly than Carol.
10. Carol follows directions more carefully than Jerry.
11. Carol dresses more neatly than Jerry.
12. Jerry gets along with people more easily than Carol.

Page 116 and 117

2. Mark stays at work the latest.
3. Mark lives the closest to the office.
4. Bill dresses the most neatly.
5. Barbara works the most carefully.
6. Bill works the most quickly.
7. Barbara works the best under pressure.
8. Barbara gets along with people the most easily.
9. Bill talks to customers the most politely.
10. Barbara works the hardest.

Make It Work

Individual answers. Some possible answers are: she works the hardest, and she gets along with people the most easily.

Page 118

2. Alberta is shorter than Olga.
3. Alberta is older than Olga.
4. Alberta dresses more neatly than Olga.
5. Alberta has more friends than Olga.
6. Alberta is prettier than Olga.
7. Alberta plays tennis better than Olga.
8. Alberta reads more quickly than Olga.
9. Alberta is more intelligent than Olga.
10. Alberta earns less money than Olga.

Pages 120

2.. I don't know where it's located. OR It's located in New York Harbor on Liberty Island.
3. I don't know what it represents. OR It represents freedom and liberty.
4. I don't know how old it is. OR It's over 100 years old.
5. I don't know where it came from. OR It came from France.
6. I don't know how it got to the United States. OR It was shipped to the United States in parts.
7. I don't know how much it cost. OR No one is sure how much it cost. (It was a gift.)

8. I don't know how high it is. OR It's 150 feet high.
9. I don't know what it's made of. OR It's made of copper. The pedestal is concrete.
10. I don't know what the statue (it's/she's) holding. OR It's holding a book or tablet in one hand and a torch or a flame in the other hand.

Pages 121
2. Do you know what it's about?
3. Do you know what time it starts?
4. Do you know what time it ends?
5. Do you know how long it is?
6. Do you know where it's playing?
7. Do you know where the Strand Theater is?
8. Do you know how far it is?
9. Do you know how long it takes to get there?
10. Do you know how much the movie costs?

Make It Work
Individual answers. Some possible answers are:
Do you know how much a meal there (at the restaurant) costs?
(Do you know what the prices are like?)
Do you know what kind of food they serve?

Page 122
2. her
3. me
4. it
5. me
6. them
7. them
8. him
9. him
10. me
11. him
12. you

Page 123
2. her, me
3. she
4. She
5. she
6. she
7. she
8. her
9. her

Make It Work
Florie: Do you want to go to the movies with Bob and me?
Marie: No, thanks. John and I are going to watch television tonight.

Page 124
2. yourself
3. myself
4. themselves
5. himself
6. herself
7. herself
8. themselves
9. himself
10. themselves

Page 125
2. themselves
3. ourselves
4. himself
5. yourself (yourselves)
6. yourself (yourselves)
7. herself
8. herself
9. myself
10. ourselves

Page 126
3. Another tie
4. Another
5. The other tie
6. The other
7. The other ties
8. The others
9. Another tie
10. Another

Page 127
2. The other
3. The others
4. The other
5. Another
6. The other
7. The others
8. Another
9. The others
10. The other

Page 128
Individual answers.

Page 129
2. to
3. to
4. —
5. —
6. for
7. for
8. —
9. for
10. to
11. for
12. —
13. for
14. to
15. —

Page 130
Individual answers using words and phrases from the charts.

Page 131
2. turn it down
3. take it back
4. fill it up
5. take it off
6. turn them off
7. call him (her) up
8. fill it out

Page 132
2. I put them on.
3. I picked it up.
4. I looked it over.
5. I wrote them down.
6. I filled them in.
7. I looked them up (in the dictionary).
8. I read it over.
9. I crossed them out.
10. I handed it in.
Individual answers.

Page 133
2. on
3. at
4. in
5. in
6. on
7. in
8. in
9. on, in
10. in, on
11. at
12. on

Page 134
2. since
3. for
4. on
5. since
6. for
7. at
8. on
9. from, to
10. at
11. on
12. for